CREATING COMPASSIONATE PLACES

CREATING COMPASSIONATE PLACES
A BABY'S BREATH

Karen Jane Patota, Founder

© 2017 Karen Jane Patota, Founder
All rights reserved.

ISBN: 0998599301
ISBN-13: 9780998599304
Library of Congress Control Number: 2017900505
Baby's Breath, A, Norristown, PA

DEDICATION TO THE BLESSED MOTHER

I dedicate this book to the Blessed Mother of God, Mary. She was my mother when people abandoned me. Her comfort and support carried me through my difficult times. She was there with compassion and strength to mother me back to God, Jesus, and the Eternal Life. I dedicate my work at A Baby's Breath to her life of humility and purity in atonement for my sins and those of the whole world. I hope that anyone who wishes to follow in my footsteps finds the grace of God through the Immaculate Heart of Mary, Mother of God through the Sacred Heart of Jesus.

*A Baby's Breath–Jeffersonville:
opened August 15, 2000, Assumption of Mary, Jubilee year*

*A Baby's Breath–Collegeville:
opened August 15, 2005, Assumption of Mary*

*A Baby's Breath–Main Line:
opened August 15, 2006, Assumption of Mary*

*A Baby's Breath–Warminster:
opened March 25, 2011, Annunciation of Mary*

*A Baby's Breath–Phoenixville:
opened May 31, 2015, Visitation of Mary*

Figure 1-A picture of the statue of Our Lady of the Assumption by Giuseppe Armani (FLORENCE company), given to us by a family friend for a wedding gift.

Special Honor and Recognition

For my family, John Patota and our children Josh, Jared, Thomas, and Victoria—thank you for sharing Mom.

Figure 2- The Patota Family

For those named and those unnamed in this book:
Thank you for your contributions in creating A Baby's Breath. Every obstacle and challenge is not an answer, but a direction. For whatever part, you have played in helping me to create A Baby's Breath, if it is not recognized in this book, God will acknowledge your contribution(s).

Thank you to Liz Cummings for helping me with the advice on how to share my personal information. The formation chapters are the spokes in the umbrella of the organization called A Baby's Breath.

Table of Contents

Introduction · xix

Book One – Founder's Formation · · · · · · · · · · · · · · · · · 1
   How Does the Baby Survive? · · · · · · · · · · · · · · · · · · · 3
   Marriage is for Life · 9
   Walking Away from Grace · · · · · · · · · · · · · · · · · · · 12
   The Path to Peace · 15
   Giving Over to God's Plan · · · · · · · · · · · · · · · · · · · 17
   Bullies · 23
   The Humility of Giving · 26
   A Compassionate Approach to Moral Teaching · · · · · · · · · · · · · 28
   Finding the Happy Balance · · · · · · · · · · · · · · · · · · · 31
   United by the Cross · 33

Book Two – The Creation of A Baby's Breath · · · · · · · · · · · · 37
   Creating our First Center in Norristown · · · · · · · · · · · · · · · · 39
      The Competition · 39
      The First "Crisis" Case · 42
      A Move Toward Accessibility—Jeffersonville · · · · · · · · · · · · 43
      Post-Abortive Volunteer · 43
      The Married Man Case · 43
      Surprise Pregnancy · 44
      Counseling Clients from Other Faiths · · · · · · · · · · · · · · · · 44
      Why the Adoption Option Should Not be Forced · · · · · · · · · 45

    A Dr. "Gosnell" Client · 45
    The Prodigal Child · 46
    A Homeschooling Client · 46
    The Late-Term Abortion Client · 47
    A Moving-Out-of-Crisis Client · 47
    Creating Our Core Services of Saving Lives and Souls—
    Pregnancy Counseling, Parenting/Prenatal Classes · · · · · · · · 48
    Training Advocates· 50
    Leadership—Keeping the Mission at Heart · · · · · · · · · · · · · · 51
    Leadership Course—Teaching Our Way · · · · · · · · · · · · · · · · 52
    Leadership—Overcoming Bullies · 53
    Finding the "Perfect Director" · 54
    A Natural Way to Plan Family—Service · · · · · · · · · · · · · · · · 54
    The Path to Peace—Blessings of Sacrifice · · · · · · · · · · · · · · · 55
Creating Our Second Center in Collegeville · · · · · · · · · · · · · · · · 58
    Planned Parenthood's Neighbor· 58
    The Angel Club—A New Way to Donate · · · · · · · · · · · · · · · · 59
    A New Way to Defend Life · 59
    Finding Mom· 60
    Overcoming Adversity—Finding the Silver Lining · · · · · · · · 61
    Overcoming the Competition· 61
    Homosexual Crisis Clients · 62
    A "Memorable" Memorial Day · 62
    Our Committed Cell Phone Holder · · · · · · · · · · · · · · · · · · · 62
    Uncommon Valor · 63
Creating Our Third Center on the Main Line· · · · · · · · · · · · · · · 64
    Why the Main Line Area?—Saint David's Center · · · · · · · · · 64
    The Bryn Mawr Experience · 64
    The Pain of the Post-Abortive Volunteer · · · · · · · · · · · · · · · 65
    Teaching Our Way of Fund-Raising· 65
    Free Professional Help· 66
    Sometimes There Is a Need for Professionals · · · · · · · · · · · 67
    A Good Professional· 68
    Fund-Raiser Naming Should Contain the Name of the
    Organization · 68

    Surviving Changes in Leadership, Competition and
    another Planned Parenthood closing · · · · · · · · · · · · · · · · · 68
    Finding a Perfect Director for Wayne · · · · · · · · · · · · · · · · 69
    The Loving our Life Service · 70
    Post-Abortive support · 70
Creating Our Fourth Center in Warminster · · · · · · · · · · · · · 72
    Finding a Founder · 72
    Interruption—The Pro-Life Competition · · · · · · · · · · · · · · 72
    A New Beginning · 73
    Lifesaving Work · 74
    Saving Lives with Our Name · 74
    The Rose Garden Service · 75
    Redirecting Clients · 75
Creating our Fifth Center in Phoenixville—Our First Home · · · · 76
    Offer for More Space · 76
    Using That Same Model for a Home · · · · · · · · · · · · · · · · · 76
    Finding a Good House Mom · 77
    Other Departures · 78
    Our First Success · 78
    The Enjoyable Workers · 78
    The Road to Independence · 79
    Our Good Leader · 79
    The Final Test of Our Model · 80

Book Three - How to Start New Centers/Services with the
A Baby's Breath Model · 81
    Keys to Development · 83
        Find your first board. · 83
        Establish the amount of funds initially available. · · · · · · · · 83
        Train your board. · 84
        Training is an ongoing process. · · · · · · · · · · · · · · · · · 84
    Opening One's Center · 85
        The initial challenge · 85
        Starting a client base · 85
        Advertising · 85

Budget · 87
    The main expenses of a center · · · · · · · · · · · · · · · · · · 87
    Establishing one fund-raiser · 87
    Financial Independence from other like-minded
    organizations · 88
    The ideal fund-raising model · 89
Maintaining a Center· 90
    Annual Leadership training · 90
    Advocate and board meetings are separate meetings
    for a reason.· 90
    Established communication · 91
    Financial reporting· 91
    Record keeping · 91
A Baby's Breath—Social Services Structure – Key Positions · · · · · 93
    Core Services Center (offering pregnancy counseling,
    prenatal/parenting classes, tutoring with a Baby Store) · · · · · 93
    Core Services Center with Ultrasound Services · · · · · · · · · · · 94
    Core Services Center with Housing Services · · · · · · · · · · · · 95
    Core Services Center with Natural Family Planning,
    Loving our Life, The Rose Garden, or Any Helpful Social
    Service Coordinators · 96
How to Create Compassionate Places- Lessons for all
faith-based social service organizations · · · · · · · · · · · · · · · · · · · 97
    Service· 98
    Mercy · 100
    Mission · 102
    Transparency· 104
    Humility · 106
    Leadership · 108
        Humility · 108
        Strength· 109
        Wisdom · 109
        Detachment of Self· 110
        Living the Lifestyle · 110
    Training Leaders · 111
    Competition · 113

    Problem Volunteers · 115
        Disrespectful of Leadership · 115
        Disregarding the Mission and Charter of the
        Organization— · 115
        Disrespecting Clients and Volunteers · · · · · · · · · · · · · · · 116
        Ineptitude · 116
        Not Showing Up · 116
    Communication · 118

Commencement of Creating Compassionate Places · · · · · · · · · · · · 121
    Ideas for Social Services Using the A Baby's Breath Model · · · · · 123
    A Baby's Breath—Social Services Structure applied –
    Key Positions · 124
    The Blessings of a Good Life · 125

Introduction

Creating A Baby's Breath was not my first choice of a career. After graduating with two degrees—a BA in applied math and a master's degree in electrical engineering—I had thought my life would be about owning my own company, creating financial success for my family, and living the American dream. I had no idea that's God's plan for my life would take such a dramatic turn. The pivotal turn for me was the birth of my first son. Seeing his beautiful face for the first time was the most euphoric moment of my life. His eyes brimmed with love for me. I felt like I had won the Olympics or had been given the most precious gift ever. At that moment, I reflected on what others may have missed. Friends of mine who had aborted their babies had missed this moment of love. It was at that point in time that I knew that God had a different plan for me, and that was to help change the devastating choice that many, many women and men have made. The thought of losing that unconditional love is what has driven me through many, many obstacles to create compassionate places where life can be chosen and supported.

In searching for direction of how to change the way the abortion choice can be made, I took a variety of turns. I joined my Respect Life group at church and found myself praying in front of an abortion clinic eight weeks after delivering my first son. What really impressed me was the nonchalance of the men escorting the mothers into the clinic. I knew what my husband's demeanor was like before and after the delivery of our son, and it was nothing like the demeanor of the men (fathers?) with the mothers. What I have found over the past seventeen years of operating A Baby's Breath is that it's not only the fathers who are nonchalant about walking into an abortion clinic, but also the mothers who view this as a health-care right. A baby in a crisis pregnancy stands in the way of perceived dreams, and the ultimate price for "freedom" is paid with an abortion.

The organization is composed of both Catholics and Protestants working toward a common mission "...to help a mother to see her child take his/her first breath."[1] Ever since I was a teenager in high school, I have been working toward communicating with Protestants from my Catholic faith. My father helped me to answer questions then, and now I communicate my faith with A Baby's Breath. There is one God, three persons—we as Christians acknowledge that. All Christians believe there is an internal transformation that takes place to acknowledge our sinfulness and need of salvation. Jesus is the path to salvation; all Christians must believe that. The confirmation of whether someone is "saved" or not is left to the churches from which they come. A Baby's Breath has written into its mission and charter that no one is to be maligned or judged for the sect of their Christian faith. We embrace the Catholic principles about contraception and abortion and work toward the solutions to a crisis pregnancy.

My organizational skills and technical education in systems engineering did not go to waste, as starting this organization required me to become familiar with how social work happens and then apply a method. The method of how we helped took about three years to develop. Initially, the method was implemented by keeping track of different pieces of information manually. An opportunity came about to take our methods and put them into a website database. It is because of this modern advance that we could grow our centers from one to five in fifteen years.

Creating compassionate places was important to me because of past experiences that needed the help of a secular therapist. I had been at a point in my life where hope was lost. I sought out and benefitted from a therapist giving me a challenge of a goal for our sessions. Once that goal

---

[1] The ellipse before our mission statement is to indicate the different reasons why someone is in a crisis pregnancy, but the mission is ...to help.

was achieved, I could move forward in my life with confidence—which is the goal of every client at A Baby's Breath. We look toward a time when life will be calm and peaceful, and every baby step is toward that end.

The model for A Baby's Breath calls for shared leadership. After five years of being both the executive director and president and everything in between, I structured the leadership of our centers into three basic positions. One was for the people who liked to work with people—the director position. The next was the general manager position—the person in charge of the finances. The last of the three parts of leadership is the donations coordinator person, the person who is keeping track of all the records—the client/volunteer records, the donations and thankyous, and anything that is tracked through the computer. These positions make up the leadership, but if one of these positions is not filled, a center can still function by having advocates who can still see clients and help volunteers become trained. If there's no general manager, a center can still function by having one main fund-raiser. The donations coordinator is a very versatile position, and we have been able to survive without a director and just a donations coordinator for extended periods of time. If there's no donations coordinator, the director can assign the various responsibilities to individual volunteers, and records and donations can be managed.

The model of A Baby's Breath has been applied to a variety of services. We have implemented a medical service for offering ultrasounds in our nonmedical centers. We have started a natural family planning service, a support group for singles called Loving our Life, a support group for adoptive parents called The Rose Garden, and most recently, have developed a housing service for our homeless pregnant clients. The services have a less restrictive demand on the general manager position in that there are no contractual obligations associated with rental agreements as in the case for centers, but the construct works in determining how that service will function. Our latest endeavor will be to apply the model to a form of welfare in a job training program. We are also expanding our services to educational funding of schools. The potential list for applying A Baby's Breath model to social service programs is endless—without government funding and free of government mandates.

KAREN JANE PATOTA, FOUNDER

The benefits of sharing one's life with others outweigh the negatives. While at times it has been a strain on the emotional status of our family, we have shown by example to our children how our faith can shape our world. We have seen a decline in the demand for abortion over the past seventeen years. We have seen a shift in public opinion about the choices for life being the more accepted way to handle a crisis pregnancy. We do not endorse single parenting, but the outcome of promiscuity should never outweigh the dignity of human life. Where there is life, there is hope.

Book One – Founder's Formation

How Does the Baby Survive?

This was my first reaction when *Roe v. Wade* was passed in 1973—I was eleven years old, and it was before my first health class, but I knew it was a magical thing when a mother became pregnant. The expression was, "You can't be a little bit pregnant." Pregnancy talk and talk in general about private matters were not readily discussed in my home. So when the law that gave us legalized abortion passed, so did my innocence of how babies were made. I thought to myself, "Did they figure out a way so that the baby doesn't get hurt?" I couldn't imagine my parents not wanting me or my siblings. I couldn't imagine life without one of my siblings, and I really wanted more of them because of how much love I received at home. My parents always told me that I was the wanted child. I was conceived after a tragic miscarriage of a third baby. My parents mourned the loss of that child, they wanted me, and they got me. I felt very special for that wanting. Now, by law the state must educate little ones younger than I was at the time abortion became legal that abortion is OK and a choice one makes when pregnant and it's not a good time. That a mother who does not want her child can simply head on into the abortion clinic with or without the consent of the father (although this is changing in some states) and have the child killed. Sometimes entire families escort the mother into the clinic to wait for their sibling to be killed at the clinic. In the span of forty-four years, in my lifetime, we have gone from, "You can't be a little bit pregnant," to "Life does not begin until the mother wants the child to be," to a family witnessing the killing of one of their own.

KAREN JANE PATOTA, FOUNDER

After *Roe v. Wade* passed, I remember reading about protests and such trying to revoke the law of the land, but my family was not active in politics other than to support candidates who supported social programs. For my family, the good was for poor people to be given support by the government. This support had been especially needed in my father's home. His family lost their mother when he was only three years old. The family of six children was left to figure out how to manage without a mother in the depths of the Depression. Their savior was the government in the form of assistance checks. The farm on which they were living was foreclosed, and they were forced to live in dire poverty without a mother. For my dad, it was a separation of church and state to have the church with its rights and wrongs, and the government for the counterbalance of corporate greed.

When I was in high school, I started to hear about girls I knew having abortions. I just assumed that their family didn't know it was wrong or just didn't care. A pregnancy in high school was obviously a problem, so an abortion would be a logical solution for someone without a faith. From my observation, there seemed to be little impact on women after an abortion. They just moved onto new relationships and forgot about the experience. For me, it was chilling to think that there was no more baby. By this time, I knew that doctors hadn't figured out a miraculous way that the baby was not harmed—they just didn't care about the baby anymore, and the law made it OK to have the baby killed.

As I moved into the work environment, I found more women who had had abortions. Some had a dramatic change of career plans afterward. Some dropped out of school. I remember hearing about a superior who had one. She did so because the baby tested positive for a genetic abnormality. She just stated matter-of-factly at a business lunch that she had had one four months into the pregnancy. By this time, the acceptance of an abortion as a "woman's right" was firmly entrenched, so no one at the lunch table where this disclosure was given had any negative reaction. I kept my opinion to myself, as I had learned that the "pro-life" position was not that popular in my business circles.

I had a lifestyle change in my twenties, and I was going back to school when I found out that a close friend had an abortion. This revelation hit me hard because we both had our Catholic upbringing. She was sharing this information because she had started to hurt. I really didn't know what to say. I was in college regrouping from my own lifestyle change and I wasn't in any position to help. I wasn't particularly political at that time, nor living within the definitions of a Christian lifestyle. I just took in the information and processed it. It was a revelation to me that families of faith had children who aborted.

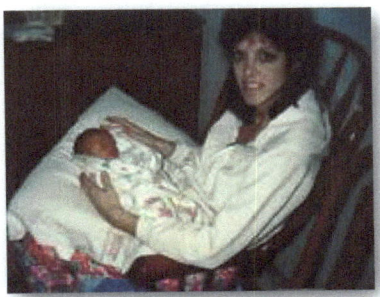

Figure 3- Holding Josh

The impact of abortion came to fruition at the pinnacle of my life—the birth of my first son. As I cradled him in my arms and peered at his beautiful face, seeing God's love in his eyes, I reflected on people I knew who had had abortions. They would never have that special first moment of seeing their child take his or her first breath. My heart was filled sorrow for them in not knowing that moment. With the birth of each of my children, I was reminded that it was a special moment that a mother has. The feeling of accomplishment and joy, the humility of being given such a great gift, and knowing that this couldn't possibly have been of my own doing. Children are a gift from God more than a burden. The joy that I had to nurture and see them grow was a reward for any sacrifice that was made to have them. They require so very little of our time and energy and yet give back with enormous return. Now that my children are almost independent of me, I finally have the time to think in retrospect about the impact of legalized abortion and our family's reaction to it. Our gift through A Baby's Breath is to help mothers, fathers, and families amid crisis pregnancies choose the path without the pain or regret of abortion. It is that compassionate perspective that went into creating A Baby's Breath.

KAREN JANE PATOTA, FOUNDER

My pro-life work did not start with founding crisis centers, but it did start immediately after my first son's birth. I joined my local church group in selling roses for life, praying in front of abortion mills, and helping pro-life candidates get elected. I helped a very pro-life woman named Peg Luksik in her two attempts at becoming the governor of Pennsylvania. I learned from her the value of using my faith in action. She was Catholic, but worked well with other Christian faiths toward a common goal. She was firm in her belief about contraception and even elevated the belief to the level of being pro-life or not. She was truly a hero in my life, and I credit a lot of what I learned as a leader working for her in her campaigns to how I managed to grow five centers including a home. Being a pro-life leader required not just the willingness to lead, but to lead by God's will.

The year that my son was born was filled with joy for my family and pain for another, as a close friend found out that her child had cystic fibrosis (CF). CF is a genetic abnormality in which the child does not secrete mucus properly, causing a lot of breathing problems in getting rid of the mucus. It was horrible to watch the parents go through their first year with every illness potentially being their child's last.

After successfully keeping their own child alive, they bravely decided to help others in finding a cure for CF. They began a fund-raiser for children with CF, and I was recruited to help with an annual silent auction. After helping for about three years, a pro-life newsletter published a list of organizations that use human embryos and aborted babies in their research—the CF Foundation was on that list. We decided that given our pro-life position, we could no longer support the effort to find a cure using human embryos and aborted babies. I thought an alternative way to support their efforts was to find a pro-life researcher. That effort involved doing a Run for Life with the proceeds going toward "pro-life medical research."

The search took nine months, and we finally found a researcher who promised not to use human embryos or aborted babies. We gave him $5,000 toward his research. Afterward, I went back to the organization that had published the list of organizations that were using babies in their research and asked about publishing an article about what we found. They asked for a picture of our researcher, and he sent me a picture of himself in front of a transgenic mouse. I asked the researcher to explain what a "transgenic" mouse was, and he replied that it was the merging of a human embryo with a mouse embryo. This was counter to the agreement that he would not use human embryos in his research.

I was devastated and decided to go in a different direction with my pro-life efforts. The lesson that I learned from this experience was to offer help only when help is requested. It was also a noted division between saving lives and souls. Sometimes the soul-saving does not equate to life-saving, and vice versa. The two concepts, saving lives and saving souls, must be considered in any pro-life initiative. Pro-life convictions are tested when it's a matter of the life of a loved one versus one that would be destroyed otherwise. In protecting all life from conception until natural death, scientific research places the lives of the unwanted human embryos and aborted babies below the intention of saving other people.

After being active in pro-life efforts for almost eight years, a crisis pregnancy hit someone close to me. A couple had tried everything to conceive and then, after two years, were finally celebrating the pregnancy. That celebration didn't last long, however. The tests that were done to assure a "healthy" pregnancy proved that the baby would have genetic issues. A valiant effort was made to save the baby, and we even offered to adopt the baby. That effort failed, and I was told if I still wanted to adopt that I could "pick the baby out of the trash." I was chilled with how little compassion was given to a baby that had been so wanted. Nine months later, almost to the day, our third son was born—to which I attribute God giving us a blessing for our efforts. The lesson that was so painful to learn from this experience was how far we had come from the concept of "a little bit pregnant" to "it's my right to kill."

The next year, our Respect Life group at church planned to do another Run for Life. This one would be the start of the A Baby's Breath organization. There were four people sitting around my kitchen table. Our attorney, who was also on the founding board, was not present, but everyone else (including my daughter, with whom I was pregnant) formed what is now the organization of A Baby's Breath. We assigned roles of secretary, treasurer, and vice president, and there was only one role left for me—that of president. In my pregnant, exuberant state, I accepted the challenge. We had our first Run for Life. It generated another $5,000. We found a 450-square-foot space to rent, and on August 15, 2000, we opened our doors.

Through the course of starting and running crisis centers, I have encountered many different cases of abortion-minded mothers and fathers. It has been through my personal experiences in knowing people who have had abortions that I was able to do so in a compassionate manner. For some crisis clients—and I would say most—the solutions worked out through our ministry have helped them to choose life. For some, they have had to see their baby in an ultrasound to choose life. For others who have not chosen life, the challenge is to help them to recover from their actions through professional counseling or spiritual retreats. The ones who knew their actions were wrong in the first place hurt the most from their decisions, and it is an indication that their conscience is still working if they hurt. However, mothers or fathers who feel hurt from their abortions are marginalized by the abortion industry and women's groups, and that makes the public disclosure of their hurt very difficult. The hurt that is identified validates that abortion is wrong for the parent as well as the child. The post-abortive parents who vehemently defend their right to choose to have an abortion are still living in denial. It is only through kindness and mercy that their hearts can be changed. People (post-abortive or not) who call themselves Christian and defend a woman's right to choose are a contradiction to their faith. God is their judge, but their beliefs do not match their faith.

MARRIAGE IS FOR LIFE

Marriage was created by God for the place where children are born. I learned this from my catechism classes. A mother and father get married and out of love the children come. A marriage is for life. This is also what I learned in my catechism class. What I didn't learn from catechism, but found out through living my life, was that the people who get married aren't perfect.

A marriage is supposed to be a happy place—but the vows say "in good times and bad." When the bad times hit, as they did with my parents' marriage, it's sometimes very unsettling for children. There's the fear of losing the warmth and happiness of all the loved ones living in one place. There's the fear of losing materials things like a house or the ability to survive financially. All these fears go with divorce for a marriage with children, but for a child with a spiritual base, these fears are compounded with the impact of breaking a vow (a commandment).

Children don't judge their parents unless they are not loved. Children provide unconditional love despite the actions of their parents. Children can see the good and ignore the bad, which is the limitation of spouses who don't get along. Children will hope against hope that things will work out and get back to the happy place they once were. It's never the case where a child will wish for a divorce, unless that child sees the option of double Christmases as a good thing. Some children just want their parents to be happy, but they don't know how to make that happen. They want their parents to be treated with respect by one another, but it's out of their control. It's a frustrating experience for a child, because the child is trying to learn conduct and respect—not teach it to his or her parents.

My first marriage did not work out. It was a painful experience to go through a divorce. I processed an annulment afterward, but I had to learn about what works in a marriage and what does not. I had stood on an altar and had taken a vow to stay married for the rest of my life. I didn't plan to get divorced, but ultimately that's what happened after three years.

For marriages without children yet, as was the case in my first marriage, the state of being married is a trial for when children do come. A spouse is looking very critically at the other spouse for how he/she will be as a parent. Will there be enough income? Will the other parent be able to help a child with the math homework? Will the spouse be a spiritual guide for the children? It's a very tenuous time for a marriage, especially if these questions are not answered before the marriage takes place.

If there's an expectation to change a spouse after marriage, then that expectation might go enormously unmet. The patterns of lifestyle will continue after marriage. Perhaps a conversion of the soul might take place, but whatever baggage there was coming into a marriage will be there after marriage.

My personal experience with marriage gave me the inspiration for wanting to do things differently in my second marriage. I had different criteria for a spouse going into my second marriage than my first: a sense of humor, my same faith, and someone who had a lot of trust in me. The other aspects of our marriage were secondary to what I had thought were the reasons for the demise of my first marriage.

Not too many of the crisis pregnancies we've seen over the course of seventeen years at A Baby's Breath have come from marriages. We've helped mostly single parents. Some were still in a relationship with the father or mother of their child, but mostly, life was chosen with the given risk of not having a relationship with the other parent. Choosing life as a single parent is a crisis at A Baby's Breath.

I began to appreciate this after having my own children. The emotional support that spouses give each other while raising children cannot be overstated. Having someone else responsible for teaching the children their faith, developing moral character and values, shaping the future generation—this is what being a parent is about. The ability for the parents to stay together in good times and bad can and will be tested. It has been only through an active participation in our faith that my marriage of twenty-five years to John Patota has been able to survive. We have withstood the trials that go with any marriage and have succeeded in staying together—peacefully.

Figure 4- John and Karen Patota - December 7, 1991

Walking Away from Grace

There was a time in my life when the choices became more difficult. It was after my parents' divorce. I had witnessed so much throughout their marriage and divorce. I had stood by my dad as his wife left him. I missed my mom very much. I had a lot of responsibility placed on me after my mom left. I had a group of girls who harassed me. My faith was weakened by all of that. I chose a boyfriend who did not treat me well. I chose him to be my husband. After that, the series of choices added up to not living a Christian lifestyle. God did not will me to go through the depths of despair, but that's what I did in *my* plan for a life. All of this has helped me in the ministry of A Baby's Breath to not judge people for their series of bad choices, but to help them on their way back to God's grace.

The help that I should have had in my walking away from grace was someone from the outside looking in to give me good advice. I was told to make bad decisions by people that I trusted, but who did not have my spiritual well-being in mind. I wish that I had had someone to lean on to protect me from hurting myself. I wish that I had had someone to say to me that there are people who wanted things from me who would not be as they said they were. I wish that I had had someone to say, "Don't do that." Everything that I wish someone would have said to me is a part of A Baby's Breath, because we care about how people feel after their decisions. We don't have the emotional attachment that our clients have to their decisions and we can advise them on what is best.

Even though none of my decisions included an abortion, I can still relate to someone who hurts from abortion, as many of our clients are post-abortive. For the post-abortive client, the hurt is an indication that their conscience still works. It is a hurt that is left from the baby. It's the only thing left in this world from the baby, so to bear that hurt is to bear the only thing left here of the baby. Of course, there's the hope of seeing the baby again in heaven, but the hurt that is experienced here in this world can be a part of the redemption for that sin. In my helping others to live a Christian lifestyle, I am helping others to not make the same bad decisions that I made, but I am hopeful that it will be a part of my redemption. For people who have had abortions, their redemption could also be to help others not to make the same mistake.

For the post-abortive parents who still don't have that hurt, my recommendation is to pray upon it. Pray for the grace needed to know the truth. If we pray the Our Father, we do seek out the people who we have hurt and ask their forgiveness. This is a good thing to do with all our sins, but especially for the instance of abortion. It is the greatest of all evils because the harm has been done to their own child. A child's love is so unconditional—it's like that of God. God loves us no matter what we do. It's only our own actions that cause that love to not be felt.

Scripture says the right frame of mind is to be not pleased with oneself.[2] It puts us in the position of trying to help our souls get to heaven. By an active and willful moving toward a position of grace, we envelope ourselves in a state of happiness. An evident way to show one's remorse (and that one is not pleased with oneself) is to help others not go down the same path. This is what I have done in the creation of A Baby's Breath. With all the tenets of A Baby's Breath, the services that we provide give the answers needed for a life of grace.

For the people who have not had an abortion, but don't voice an opinion about it or the people who make that decision, the question is whether they would allow anyone—including a loved one—to hurt himself or herself. Would they want someone to slam a hammer on his or her finger or to jump off a bridge? For many post-abortive clients, this

---

2 "For the flesh desires what is contrary to the Spirit, and the Spirit what is contrary to the flesh. They are in conflict with each other, so that you are not to do whatever you want." (Galatians 5:17)

is how they feel. They hurt from their decision and many times they feel like aborting themselves. It's only because the media has portrayed abortion as a choice between a mother and doctor—it is not. It is a choice between a parent and a child, grandparent/parent and child, aunt/uncle/parent and child, best friend/parent and child—everyone who would have recognized the child as a part of their loved one's life would be hurt by the decision of the parent to abort. Abortion hurts more than just the parent of the aborted child. It hurts the surrounding community of love that would have encompassed the aborted child's world.

There is a commonality among parents who have aborted: they have people around them who influenced them to have the abortion. If this is the case, the post-abortive parent is the victim of bad advice. He/she must bear the brunt of the hurt, but the culpability of the decision to abort falls on the people who have influenced the decision. For this group of post-abortive parents, the hurt is quite sad, in that they have people around them who have not done right by them. The influencers are the ones who need redemption for not helping the person in crisis to make the right decision. Planned Parenthood often is that influence, isolating their abortion clients from their network of support. It is for this reason that Planned Parenthood and other abortion providers are so evil in their operation. To not fully allow a mother or father to understand the consequences of their action is their evil nature.

Coming back from the decision to abort is not a closed-ended process because one can never quite recover from that decision. The act of abortion cannot totally be undone. The baby will never be here. Post-abortive parents must own their decision and then decide how they can possibility recover from that decision. Some who have not sought counseling go into a series of decisions that make up for the abortion decision. Some will immerse themselves in a lifestyle that removes the hurt, transfers the guilt, and does not directly help their healing or slow the propagation of abortion. What would be best for post-abortion parents' healing is sharing the negative consequences of abortion so that others may learn from their mistakes. This is my hope for A Baby's Breath—to help others not make the same mistake.

The Path to Peace

Peace is not a term associated with crisis because it is the opposite. For anyone who has lived through a time when things are not peaceful, it can be a time that one would rather forget. We have a lot of people who have come to A Baby's Breath in crisis, and it's not a time to dwell upon past hurts, but to focus on the plan to move forward, a path to peace.

I learned this from my own experience with crisis when my first marriage broke up. It required the help of a professional who helped me to help myself. He had me identify the goals that I would need to satisfy in order to be considered "healed." While the goals that I established were tangible, the emotions that surrounded these goals were very difficult. I had built up so many emotions about things and people that I wasn't aware I had. It was all bottled up inside, but when I would discuss specific issues that did not really come with an agenda, the outpouring of these emotions helped to solidify the decisions that I ultimately had to make.

This is the approach that we take at A Baby's Breath. A crisis pregnancy is an emotional time. There's uncertainty about many different decisions—to parent or to choose the adoption path. To find a new job or to go back to school. To stay with the father or mother of the baby or to find a respectful relationship. These situations have unique circumstances, but all of them must be decided and owned by the client—not by the advocate.

From my own personal situation, my crisis was mirroring the relationship that I had with God. It was out of step. My counseling didn't need to point that out, because the state of my emotions was the telling. God doesn't choose chaos—we choose it. The counseling was very helpful and gave me closure at the end of our sessions that helped me to know which direction to take. While the next steps were going to be a challenge, I was mentally ready to embrace my new life. There was one more benefit to addressing the emotions attached to my decision-making, and that is that I never looked back with regret. I moved forward with my life and had closure on knowing whether I was making the wrong decision.

This is the failure of the abortion "choice." There are no second chances at choosing an abortion. There's potential healing, but there's no resurrecting the baby. A mother who chooses the adoption path has the benefit of knowing that her child has been given life. Even though it might seem like a loveless choice, it is loving the child twice to choose to give the gift of child to another parent while giving the gift of life to the child. Reconciliations can always take place, and that child will always know who gave him or her life. The adoption choice is a loving way to parent a child.

Single parenting a child requires special help in finding the resources needed to provide for the child. There's a lot of planning that needs to take place for a single parent—plans that go best when there are two people to make those decisions. Single parents at A Baby's Breath set goals and move toward them, but the balance between family and work demands every ounce of patience from the single parent. The advocates at A Baby's Breath have special gifts that allow the mother or father to think about goals while having their emotions heard. The advocates are not necessarily trained social workers, but they do provide the critically needed support in times of crisis.

Giving Over to God's Plan

My Confirmation was the official transformation of my soul to God's victory, but it wasn't a lifelong state of mind. Instead, it was a gradual but willful desire to do what is right and be at peace with God's plan. When I was in an art class in my public middle school, I made a Crucifix for a project. My hands molded what was, at the time, most inspirational. In that same art class, a girl came into school from another. She looked lost and beaten down, so I struck up a conversation with her. I didn't think anything about it, but my teacher pulled me aside to give me accolades for that gesture. I was operating off an internal moral compass of grace at that point. I was too young to realize the significance of the situation. I just liked helping people feel more comfortable. I didn't realize at the time that this is what Jesus taught us to do in our actions to be kind and merciful.

Later in my teens, when my life started to crumble with my parents' divorce, I became lost myself. I pulled myself back on the path, but it wasn't before making mistakes that had me wanting more peace in my life. The sacraments were always a good way to feel better, and that's what I've always done. Grace was still being offered to me, but I did not respond in the right way. I was still not able to see what logical and right decisions needed to be made for my life. I ended up marrying my first boyfriend for reasons that still do not make sense. He wasn't the right choice for my husband. God doesn't give exact answers—He gives us free will. It wasn't sinful to make the choice to marry him; it was just the wrong choice. My bad marriage led to other mistakes, and so by the time

KAREN JANE PATOTA, FOUNDER

I could make the right decision to leave, it nearly cost me my life. My experience with my first marriage and other bad choices helped me to understand how the clients who we help at A Baby's Breath find themselves pregnant. What seems like the right thing to do in the moment ultimately could be the wrong decision. Stepping out of that situation is not always easy, but with the grace of God, anything is possible.

Getting out of my first marriage took about five years. What I should have done is gracefully given over all the hard-earned assets acquired in the first marriage, but I didn't. I waited until life was "perfect" before marrying for the second time. I finished two degrees, found a person more suited to my ideal of a "perfect" husband, and then acquiesced to a second marriage. I didn't give myself a chance to separately decide with God's grace, and it has been a challenge to redeem myself from all those previous decisions. Sharing our clients' journey out of crisis requires a lot of patience, and only someone who has experienced how difficult is it to reroute back onto God's plan can appreciate the time it takes for souls to change their lifestyle. By the time I realized how wrong I was in my choices, I was embedded in a trail of decisions that took years to undo.

My challenges with choosing God's plan have helped me to minister to other lost souls. I can understand when we see clients for the first, second, and third time in a crisis pregnancy. Sometimes it takes a soul many trials by God to realize that His plan works the best. Sometimes we don't realize that God is trying to teach us by what happens in our lives. This was evident by an experience with a client who came to our center in the middle of the night. She was being beaten by her partner. She was a methadone client, and her family had had enough of her bad decisions, so they refused to help anymore. We tried to find an abuse shelter for her, and I drove her twenty-five miles away and gave her my last twenty dollars. She then took the money and got a taxi back to the home with her partner. We don't enable violence, so we had to separate ourselves from her until she started making better decisions. The evil of drug-induced clients is that they are completely separated from their right conscience. The drugs make their decisions. Over the seventeen years of A Baby's Breath's existence, the addicts remain our most difficult clients to help. They render themselves incapable of choosing God's plan, and that's what makes addiction of any kind evil. Having the ability to choose God's plan requires the grace of free will.

Some clients who are in the throes of crisis are blinded to which path to take. They are living day to day with sin, which does not lend itself to clear thinking. A Baby's Breath provides loving souls who have seen or been in the same place as our clients. They have helped their children or other loved ones navigate through bad situations. Advocates at A Baby's Breath advocate God's plan, but allow the clients to emotionally journey back to the right choices. They would never allow clients to leave our centers thinking it was OK to abort or to choose contraception or to have their tubes tied. We have had volunteers who have come to A Baby's Breath thinking that they could ignore some of our principles, because the clear majority of Catholics believe that contraception is OK. One way or the other, we seem to find out what they have done, and soon they are no longer volunteers. Volunteers have free will too, and sometimes it is a challenge to see a mother in crisis led to make a decision that goes against our principles—meaning, a recommendation to get a tubal ligation. What is wrong about this recommendation is that it does not solve the real problem in our client's life. She is allowing herself to be used for a purpose that separates life and love. The feeling of hopelessness in a person who is used is caused by their lifestyle, and a baby that emanates from an unchaste lifestyle is not the problem. We hold firm to the belief that artificial contraception propagates more crisis pregnancies instead of preventing them.

My commitment to God's plan was reaffirmed with the birth of my first son. Seeing his beautiful face was so inspirational to me that I wanted to make his world as special as he did mine. I had never felt the unconditional love like I had when I first held him. I believe many mothers and fathers have had that conversion or the start of their moving back to God's plan at their first child's birth, and that is why we should always support pregnancy, even if it comes at a time that is not the best. The direction is moving forward—not backward. A child's sweet unconditional love is a reminder of God's love for us. God can always improve us if we are open to His help.

Sometimes, our minds get cluttered to the point where we start reaching out for comfort where it has potential for harm. This has happened to me over the course of my life. Instead of relying upon God's divine help, I reached for human help. The problem is that that kind of human help can get corrupted and self-serving. God doesn't sugarcoat things. If one is doing wrong, God will allow one to know it. God is perfect. Humans are not. Unless another human being has been designated as a spiritual authority, one cannot expect their advice to be pure. A young, vulnerable woman in a troubled marriage might seek advice from her boss, and then the trouble begins. We have had crisis pregnancies from extramarital relationships, and it is especially difficult to witness. The child is the innocent victim in an ill-conceived relationship. Both parties are held accountable for a mutually consenting relationship, but the child is the victim. He or she is expecting two parents and instead has the memory of a bad relationship. A woman who allows herself to be in an extramarital affair is asking for misery for herself and her potential child. Understanding that a baby that arises from an extramarital affair is not the problem has been helpful for me to understand why lost souls who have come to A Baby's Breath have landed in a crisis pregnancy. The mothers and fathers who have had their trust misplaced, have been abandoned and are choosing life are the ones who especially need our emotional support and comfort.

My second marriage has been a spiritual journey in and of itself. We celebrated our twenty-fifth year this past year. We have four beautiful children, who came as a blessing to our commitment to marriage. Marriage for me is not so much about the person to whom I am married, but the person that I've become since being married. It has allowed me to be a mother and show my love of life for God in taking care of my children's needs and their spiritual nurturing, and ultimately has resulted in four more souls to love, serve, and honor God. I never had to show them any graphic pictures of aborted babies for them to understand that abortion was wrong. They just knew that Mom's time spent on saving babies and helping mothers, fathers, and families was important. I didn't plan on sacrificing my entire job earning potential to the pro-life movement, but since my husband made enough money for two incomes, I felt that I was given a special gift that I could give back. With our budget, we could have five centers, including a home and no compensation for a CEO/executive director or we could have one center/home which would finance the costs of one center/home and the salary of a CEO of one executive director. I chose to have the five centers including a home to offer places where mothers, fathers, and families could find answers and real help in their choices for life. It's not been easy, especially in the college years with the rising cost of Catholic education, but I can look back and tell my children and my God that I did everything that I could to save the little ones and their parents from a disastrous decision.

As for my marriage and what has allowed its endurance of twenty-five years, I will quote from our current vice president, Mike Pence, who said this to his wife as they got married, "God is number one in our marriage." That same thought has allowed me to accept the imperfections in the human being that I married, John Patota, and he mine. He has been an ardent supporter and joined in our sacrifice of my earning potential to offer my services toward the administration of A Baby's Breath. He has shared the joys and burdens of raising four children. He wanted more—not less—children, and so it was all of me that he wanted, not just the parts that were especially joyful.

Figure 5- Crucifx made in my art class

Bullies

I didn't think I was learning anything when I was in the middle of being bullied in high school, but those lessons were extremely valuable in my adult life, particularly in my vocation for starting crisis centers. In high school, the objective of the bullies was to intimidate me from dating my boyfriend. My nemesis and her gang proceeded to berate me at the restaurant where I worked, let the air out of my tires, and write upsetting things on my desk and around school to the point where going to school was torture. I missed the most school one can miss without getting expelled. The goal of bullying is to make someone feel small so that the bully can feel big. It's a very evil practice, because this is what the Evil One does to drag us down his path. Sin and licentious behavior will cause us to feel small and worthless, while God and His Mercy pull us back to grace.

When I first started working for God after my son was born, I encountered bullies from the pro-choice side. They were adamant about their choice belonging to the mother of the baby exclusively. From the political side to the social spectrum, the choice for abortion was revered as essential to their line of thinking, and anyone stepping in front of that liberty was not respected. At the polls, where I would distribute literature for pro-life candidates, I experienced the disdain for someone who opposes a "woman's right to choose." In a social setting among people from both sides, the pervading expectation was that it was a private matter between a doctor and the woman. The brunt of the bullying on the pro-choice side, however, fell on the unborn baby—who had only pro-life people to defend him or her. Since the law was on the pro-choice side, the main effect of the bullying could remain between the pro-choice person and the unborn baby, so the victory for now is on anyone who considers legal abortion OK—we shall see how diplomatic pro-choice people are when the rights for the unborn are overturned.

I have to say that the most vitriolic bullying that I have experienced in my personal and professional pro-life vocation has not been from the pro-choice side, but the pro-life side. In my efforts to start A Baby's Breath, I faced hindrances instead of help in the areas of training and funding and accessibility. If I wasn't part of a certain faith base, I was not able to join a network of crisis pregnancy centers. If didn't become a specific crisis pregnancy center organization (as we were in choosing to be A Baby's Breath), other centers tried to sabotage our efforts to help mothers and fathers in crisis pregnancies. One national pro-life group put up on their website that people were not supposed to take their abortion-minded clients to centers with the word "baby" in their name. We had an entire group of people leave a board at one center because they wanted to take "baby" out of our name. The battle for clients and volunteers has gotten so competitive that billboards have been erected one mile from our busiest center, directing clients and volunteers to call a center twenty miles away. One volunteer said she called the number on the sign six times before finally just walking into our center to find out how to volunteer.

I found bullies internally as well. One volunteer kept our database for six months, so we couldn't send out our newsletter. We had another volunteer leader who raised up our firewall, so we couldn't login to our system. We had to pay a software expert $5,000 to fix it. We've had people who have come to help with our fund-raisers whose personal demands outweighed the common goals of our mission. We've had volunteers who have come to help, but instead demand that their issues be dealt with according to their way and leave abruptly and nastily because they don't get their way. I added a line to our volunteer agreement to specifically ask volunteers who needed to leave to please not send global e-mails so not destroy an organization that is trying to do good – this has not always been successful and at times our organization has been hurt by the very people who have come to help.

All these issues, which seemed overwhelming at the time, only made us stronger in the end. As the founder, I felt very distraught by so many obstacles over the years, but I think back to the training God made me go through in my early years that made me readied for the battle. I've read enough saint books to know that competition among faith-based organizations is common going back to the time of Saint Theresa of Avila. She wrote in *The Book of Foundations* that she was sued by the Augustinians for reaching over into their territory for sponsors. Saint Theresa has been a great inspiration for me in many ways. Her spiritual ways were close to those we use to help our clients. Saint Theresa was very keen on allowing God to be the victor in her ministry. This has been my solace in times of outward aggression toward our organization. God has fire-tested us, and we have withstood the battles to become a haven for thousands of mothers, fathers, and families in crisis pregnancies.

The Humility of Giving

The assumption about giving help at A Baby's Breath is that there should be no expectation of reward or public recognition for this work. One who comes to volunteer at A Baby's Breath should feel no greater stature than the clients being served, or else the value of what is being done is lost. If one cannot relate to the need for help, one will never understand why we do what we do. If one has never needed anyone's help, one cannot expect to give that help with the right humility. Anger and forceful methods are not a part of how we help our clients at A Baby's Breath. The clients who come for help at A Baby's Breath are either in great need or don't know how much need they have. For some, it's for the material items; for others, it's for the spiritual guidance. We serve them both at A Baby's Breath.

My understanding of helping those in need didn't really come from my own home, since we were well taken care of materially and there was always enough food to eat. There were, however, times of spiritual need, especially during the time of divorce. In my parents' home, when my mom left, my dad took us to Mass. I could feel the love of God in that time of need. Later, when my first marriage broke up, my mom could offer a place of compassion. It was those two experiences that best describe how we help at A Baby's Breath. We are serving the material needs with compassion, as well as the spiritual needs of our clients who are lost.

Clients who feel that they are on a conveyor belt of service will not feel loved or individually served. A Baby's Breath provides one-on-one counseling that could only be afforded through volunteer advocates and leaders. It takes many hours to accommodate the great emotional needs of our clients. Their goals and motivations are all individual. For those who are ready to accept our type of help, the transition from crisis to stability and peace is an easy path. For many, there are challenges and blockages to understanding what peace is. We help them to define that path. For my own path out of crisis, I needed to identify goals for myself that were going to be there when my crisis was over. This is critically important in order to avoid creating a lifetime of dependency on therapy. When I went to a therapist after my first marriage broke up, he asked me to define my goals. His interest was in my well-being and not his monetary benefit. We take the same approach at A Baby's Breath with our clients, having them think out their path out of crisis. We are not interested in creating a conveyor belt of clients, but a culture of life.

Many of the volunteers who are drawn to help at A Baby's Breath are also in need of guidance, but from a different perspective. The difference between a client and a volunteer is that one is in an out-of-control crisis, and the other is in a managed crisis. When A Baby's Breath was first created, I was in managed-crisis mode. I was expecting my fourth baby, home-schooling two children and mothering four. I could open and start an organization only with my husband's help. I could manage my crises. We had bills to pay, and children who needed our care. My goal was to see them into college, provide their spiritual upbringing, pay off the house, and live life. All was possible with God's and my husband's help.

A Compassionate Approach to Moral Teaching

I had been confirmed when I was thirteen years old. It was the same year a close family friend was killed in a car accident. She was beautiful and nice and didn't mind the conversing with a thirteen-year-old sister of her best friend. Seeing her beautiful body dressed in a prom gown in a coffin was so distressing for me. I had never been so attached to anyone who died before. It was a powerful moment for me to digest what I had learned about death from my confirmation lessons. Was she in heaven yet? Why hadn't God saved her from this? She had been so nice and pretty and the whole rest of her life was taken away.

This is how I approached why it was so wrong to have an abortion. What a tragic loss it was for the mother to not see the beautiful baby resting in her arms. How unfair it was for the father who could not protect his child from harm in an abortion. The grandparents, aunts, and uncles miss out on seeing their relatives grow up and be a part of the family (what family doesn't like birthday parties, first Holy Communion parties, weddings?)—all that is taken away with one person's choice. The friends, who would be sharing children of the same age and watching with joy at their accomplishments, have their joy taken from them with only the mother's choice. The prospective adoptive families, who could parent a child and take any financial burden away, have their future happiness with the child to be aborted destroyed. The baby, whose future could hold so much promise and hope, now becomes a bitter memory—and although "healing" does exist for any post-abortive mother or father, nothing can replace the warmth of a child's love. The future of an unborn child rests with the good graces of the mother (and sometimes the father in some states). God gave everyone free will to decide to do what's right or wrong, so it is not God who chooses to abort, taking away all the joy and happiness of the unborn baby.

In the seventeen years of running A Baby's Breath centers, I have seen how the abortion decisions come to be, and it's usually not the case that the mother is acting defiantly alone—sometimes she is, but most times she's not. Usually the mother is unduly influenced while in a crisis. A baby who is conceived at time when it's not good to be pregnant places an inordinate amount of stress on the mother. She is worried about where to live, how to finish her education, and what her family and friends will think of her if she's pregnant—maybe for the second or third time. Therefore, as difficult as it is to watch a mother return in a crisis pregnancy, we do not judge her for that return. We continue to work on the lifestyle as God continues to work on us through compassion and Mercy.

It would be easier if the law of the land outlined the right and wrong thing to do in abortion decision, but our faith guides us with the Ten Commandments. The Judeo-Christian commandment is "Thou Shalt Not Kill," and yet, we have had many churchgoing families who struggle with the answer. Their thoughts are misguided from the absolute truth of the sanctity of human life to one of relative goodness. Just because a pregnancy comes at the wrong time does not make it right to terminate that pregnancy. We've had parents who think their children's right to choose and abort comes before their children's duty to choose life.

Of course, babies should come from marriage. This is God's plan, because it makes it so much easier to finance their well-being and to take care of a baby's needs. The mistake is not the baby. The mistake is usually promiscuity. Parents who know that their children are sexually active should not be surprised by a crisis pregnancy. Contraception is not always foolproof. We've had clients who have had their tubes tied come to us in a crisis pregnancy. If one is going to be sexually active, one had better prepare for the occurrence of pregnancy. Pregnancy does not necessarily imply parenting. Choosing life should imply either parenting or choosing adoption. I've never understood how a client could say "I can't choose life because I wouldn't want my child to think I didn't love him/her." What about killing communicates love? Choose to give a child to a childless couple if you cannot parent.

A complication arises when the child is wanted by one parent and not the other. If it's the father of the baby who wants to parent and the mother considers adoption, then the struggle for parenting begins. If a child is parented, the other parent must financially support the baby as well. The law of the land can and should protect a baby to be born, but it cannot protect two people who should not be conducting themselves as married when they are not.

Finding the Happy Balance

When I accepted the challenge of starting an organization, I submitted my resignation from every other board that I could have possibly volunteered on. I was not able to offer help to my children's schools, their sports teams, even positions at church—instead, this organization was my contribution to my children, my society, and my church. Even with that concession, there were times of stress, especially in the home-schooling years when I thought to myself, "Is this worth it?" It's taken me seventeen years to realize it, but yes, it has been worth it.

There are some people who gravitate toward the other areas, but it takes very special people to volunteer at A Baby's Breath. The leaders and volunteers must exemplify the mission and charter of the organization. Not everyone on sport teams or at school or even at church has that kind of standard. I had to recognize that from the beginning, when only four people sitting around my kitchen table were answering the call to start a crisis center in my community. Jesus mentioned this in the scripture: "The harvest is plenty but the workers are few" (Matt. 9:37).

The structure of A Baby's Breath fits into busy family life. From the beginning, I could not be a director forty hours/seven days per week. I was a director for two and a half hours per week. One might have just thrown in the towel, but I didn't, and now we have five centers and a home. I didn't stress about not being a perfect leader because we were meeting the needs of our clients. The only time I stressed was when I felt my children were not getting enough attention, specifically with their homeschooling. When things came to a head, I placed them all in school and prayed for their protection.

Each child's needs were different. If one decides to parent with a one-size-fits-all strategy, one will find that the shoe doesn't fit all. What's important is to try to love uniquely and timely. I prioritized with the oldest getting the most of my attention until he was more independent and he could help me with the rest. With my second getting ready to graduate from college, and third starting this next year, my strategy seems to have worked. They all go to church regularly, even at college. They all have a moral foundation.

When my husband and I married twenty-five years ago, we didn't set out to devote our whole lives to A Baby's Breath, but that's what we did. Looking back, it was well worth all the sacrifices and burdens, but we didn't know what we were accepting for our lives. We just trusted God that we had chosen well.

United by the Cross

Right after receiving my Confirmation, I was tested by a group of Fundamentalists on my knowledge of Sacred Scripture. I was asked if I was "saved." I really didn't know. I thought if one obeyed the Ten Commandments, received the sacraments, and believed in the tenets of the Apostles' Creed, the judgment was up to God. I thought once I died, my soul would be in a state of purgatory until it would receive the eternal reward of heaven. The fundamentalists told me that they believed that all I had to do was ask to be saved, to ask Jesus into my heart, and then Salvation happened forever and ever. It was a different way to believe that there was an immediate transfer of my soul into heaven, but it sounded too good to be true. I went to a prayer group meeting, and when I was asked for my intentions and said, "My grandfather who had passed," they laughed. I didn't really know if there was a common ground until starting A Baby's Breath.

I had other friends who were also Christian, but not Catholic, and there was a lot of commonality in terms of knowing right from wrong. I believe that common Wisdom was that of the Holy Spirit. I believe that what we had in common far outweighed our differences because it is through the Holy Spirit and the Trinity that can know, love and serve God—the way that Catholics believe heaven is attained.

There are some Catholics who still don't believe in the teachings of the Catholic catechism, and they are not the ones who come to volunteer at A Baby's Breath. They are the ones who stand back and allow abortion to stay legal and do not do anything to prevent a mother or father in crisis from making a mistake.

Working with Peg Luksik on her political campaign was my first experience with how to bridge the gap between Christians. She didn't dilute the tenets regarding contraception and abortion but held firm to them. She knew her scripture and could win over Bible Christians who might think that Catholics don't study the Bible. We do, but it's according to the Liturgy of the Word. There are Bible groups at Catholics churches as well that teach the Word of God as it is written, but the scripture, "This is my Body" is interpreted differently. Some Christians believe the Word is the bread (the Body), and Catholics believe is it the Transubstantiation of the bread into the Body (the Eucharist), but both require the digestion of God's teaching. Catholics believe that God continues to reveal himself in other forms of written documents and is reflected in the lives of the saints. Saints are people who demonstrate lives of holiness and have been canonized.

There are many saints who are in heaven besides the ones who are famous. My grandmother on my mother's side was a holy woman. She would pray her rosary every night before bed. She survived her husband's death for thirty years, and her Catholic faith held her strong until the end. The main difference between Catholics and other Christians is how one attains heaven. Catholics believe we are saved by our response to grace in the way that we live. We also believe that souls who have passed can be helped by the souls still alive to pray for them into heaven. If we are all working toward saving lives and souls, then the grace that God gives will be sufficient for all Christian souls to be saved.

Born-again Christians believe in a metanoia (change of heart) to become saved. Catholics do as well, but it is not a once-and-done deal. How well we maintain the status of our metanoia is for God to judge, but a more peaceful existence, one that replicates heaven, is attained by the willful choosing of God's plan.

A Baby's Breath is Catholic and Christian. We have this base so that one does not have to become Catholic to work on our mission. One just needs to respect the mission and charter, which is in keeping with the magisterium of the Catholic Church. We don't require a confirmation by the volunteers who help our clients, and we don't teach Catholicism to our clients unless they are already Catholic. We help clients of all faiths in choosing a path that is right in a Catholic–Christian direction. It has been a great way to teach the truth about my Catholic faith.

Figure 6- Four Generations with Victoria

Book Two – The Creation of A Baby's Breath

Creating our First Center in Norristown

Our Norristown center didn't start out in Jeffersonville, where our current Norristown center is located, but in a 450-square-foot space in Fairview Village, which is geographically close to Norristown, but it was not accessible by public transportation. We were offered this location by a fellow church member at a reasonable rate. We opened on August 15, 2000. The space was large enough for a reception room and a room for counseling, but not much else. My husband was away for three weeks when we opened. I had to hire a babysitter so that I could sit in the space and manage the new volunteers. Verizon went on strike, so I went and purchased our first cell phone. Some of the new volunteers used the phone to sit and make personal calls. It was my hope that once the center was built, the "perfect" director would volunteer herself, and I would be able to get back to my happy life of just managing four children. That never happened. Instead, the Patota family learned to manage without a mom on occasion, and my husband would have to share his wife with many, but God got the priority in our lives. Babies would be saved and lives transformed through the sacrifice toward a devotion to life.

The Competition

A Baby's Breath was started in a town that had a Catholic Social Service (CSS) office, but it was not specifically dedicated toward helping mothers, fathers, and families in crisis pregnancies. The other form of pro-life help was a hotline, but other than that, the next closest center was twenty-five miles away. Initially, I had thought that our center would be a duplicative effort with the local CSS, but then a representative stopped by. She looked at our brochure, which detailed a baby in utero, and her remark gave me pause. She said she couldn't judge someone with five kids who had one abortion and then chose life and then had another abortion. It was a real case that she had handled, and she said she'd almost been fired for it. Wow, I knew then why our center had to exist. We would never allow a mother to leave our doors thinking that it was OK to have an abortion.

The other competition that started from the beginning was an organization that did a lot of political lobbying, praying in front of abortion clinics, and sidewalk counseling, but they had no office or center for directly helping mothers, fathers, and families. I had expected our project to be endorsed or supported by the local pro-life organization, but instead was given another obstacle in the creation of our centers. Their center was to be built in the same town. There is no rationale for pro-life organizations competing with one another, but the loser is the client who needs our help, or the volunteer who wants to do God's pro-life work. This became an issue in the form of financial support. The other organization, who organized rose sales at most of the parishes, did not want to share the support they received on the parish doorsteps, so we were forced to create a system of support that did not interfere with their ability to get direct support from parishes. It only made us stronger in the end.

After choosing not to be a certain crisis pregnancy center organization, they would limit their help to lending us a training manual and a trainer who volunteered to teach our new volunteers for one day how to counsel a client not to have an abortion.[3] This was extremely helpful to all of us who had no experience in directly helping mothers and fathers in crisis pregnancies. Also, when we decided not to be a specific organization, one of the key supporters left, because in his mind, we were dismissing the good name that had saved so many lives. As a board,

---

3 The trainer from the other crisis pregnancy center said that it was an organizational policy not to help any other organization if they decided not to be that organization, but she personally felt it was in her good conscience to help us know the basics of crisis counseling.

we decided that it was more important to have our mission and charter stand for who we were and how we wanted to help. We didn't want to limit the number of services that we could provide, and we wanted to take a stand against contraception. This was specifically not a part of the other organization's mission and charter and totally separated the two conversations. *The Gospel of Life* by Pope John Paul II states the connection by saying that contraception is the root of abortion, so in our mission and charter we state that the contraception mentality separates life and love and creates more unplanned pregnancies. From our experience, most of the clients we see are on some form of birth control. Obviously, methods are important, so we stood our ground on creating a new organization. We also had an issue with financial competition with this organization because their method of support was to claim a church as theirs, and no other pro-life organizations could benefit from that church. They had a huge budget for each center, which is comparatively significantly larger than our center budgets. They had a goal to own property, which is not a priority with A Baby's Breath. We prefer long-term lease agreements and to avoid the burden of owning property.

After our center had grown to more than three centers, I was curious to see how our center fared in the Internet searches for crisis pregnancy help.[4] I went to one of the websites that advertises crisis pregnancy centers to search for pregnancy help in the zip code of our oldest center, and the search pointed me to a center twenty-five miles away. I tried to get our centers listed in that network, and I found that I could not because of our base. The base refers to which religion our organization vouched for in its mission and charter. I became familiar with the idea of base and the term "statement of faith" when a volunteer from one of the competitors came to volunteer with us. We have a mission and charter that allow for Christians of different sects to work together. This volunteer helped us to include a tenet that made her happy, which was to declare that Jesus was the path to heaven. The Statement of Faith document required organizations to affirm that the Bible was the only inspired word of God, which dismissed any revelations since the Apostles, including those of our patron saint, Saint Therese of Lisieux.

---

4 There are pregnancy networks on-line who will direct a client to a specific center.

The other competition came in the form of a dominating national pro-life organization that insisted we show graphic imagery to help save babies. We subscribed to a more compassionate form of education that did not utilize graphic imagery. We didn't think showing this imagery saved lives and we did not want to further the damage done by the abortion industry in showing the results of an abortion. We didn't think it was respectful to the child who was killed and the parent who might later try to seek reconciliation with the church. It was a divisive issue that would lead to a key volunteer leaving us because we didn't allow it.

The First "Crisis" Case

It was Holy Thursday, nine months to the date since we had opened our doors. We had been training our volunteers according to a cryptic model of another organization's training manual. We also had also been procuring clients from a local family practice to be able to help directly with clients, but this was our first abortion-minded client. We knew the first "crisis" client would come, but it was amazing that that case came on Holy Thursday. As my family sat down to dinner, we were interrupted by a call on the center cell phone. The client needed help immediately, as her partner was considering an abortion. I called an older advocate in to help. She was a religious woman who came to the center with her saint relics. She rushed to the center, and I waited in the waiting room while she attended the clients. The couple were homosexual, but one of the clients, the client who was pregnant, was living in a house of prostitution. She had had an affair with a male and had become pregnant. She wanted to choose abortion, but her partner wanted to parent the child. The advocate was personally in favor of showing the client a picture of an aborted baby, but we had a policy of not doing that, so she acquiesced and proceeded to defend life without graphic pictures. The battle for the baby's life was won, and no graphic pictures needed to be shown. Amen. It was our first successful "save." That baby is now prayerfully seventeen years old.

A Move Toward Accessibility—Jeffersonville
We moved to the center to Jeffersonville in September of 2001, one week before 9/11. It was a large, beautiful space that our landlord transformed into a comfortable, welcoming space where we could expand our services from just giving things away to providing real, quality services. A Baby Store was constructed on a rainy Super Bowl weekend. My husband and I wove together lattices to form the walls. Baby items were picked up off the floor and organized into bins so that the moms could see the items and choose what she needed for her baby. The generosity of our donors and volunteers was overwhelming. It was a perfect location to grow our tiny center into what it is today—the most active center that we have.

Post-Abortive Volunteer
We had a woman come to our first training and leave halfway through in tears. I didn't understand at the time, but later she came to speak to me privately. She said she had had an abortion with her first child. She then had more children with an abusive husband. She got divorced from her husband and was working through the layers of post-abortive syndrome. She had been to confession many, many times and yet still could not shake the guilt. She then went to a Rachel's Vineyard[5] retreat. She wanted to help, but did not feel capable in a situation where a baby's life was on the line. I gave her a key to the center and she seemed to find comfort in just being there. I ran into her years later, and her daughter had a crisis baby. She seemed to glow in helping her daughter in choosing life.

The Married Man Case
One of our advocates was a nurse with beautiful blue eyes. She was a spiritual person. She had been one of the four people sitting around my kitchen table when we first began, and her crisis call came from a woman who was having an affair with a married man. The client came in with the married boyfriend. The nurse wasn't quite sure how the session had gone, so after the session was over, she got down on her knees and

---
5 Rachel's Vineyard (www.rachelsvineyard.org)

KAREN JANE PATOTA, FOUNDER

prayed. Nine months later, the mom brought her baby in to show her that she did in fact choose life. This was the first of many cases where we didn't know about a client's decision until months later. It always gives us hope to think that life was chosen, even if the client didn't affirm it in the visit.

Surprise Pregnancy

We also opened a center in 2003 in Norristown Borough. The space was donated and we just covered expenses. We closed the center in 2006 because the space was not functional and the location was treacherous for our volunteers. We had a volunteer who was an intern for us at Norristown. She found herself pregnant in the ninth month. I had never heard of such a thing, but apparently, if a mother is very skinny, her pregnancy could be masked. I then became aware of the irregular menstrual cycles of very skinny people. She was not a client, she was a volunteer, but just as the case with many of our volunteers, they can help us learn about crisis pregnancies. Fortunately, her parents supported her choice for life and embraced and shared her crisis.

Counseling Clients from Other Faiths

We've had more than one case of where the mother or father believes in reincarnation. This is a challenge in advocating for life, because in this case, there is no spiritual consequence to the choice for abortion—the same baby comes back in a different body. One highly educated couple came to our Norristown center and asked to see a graphic picture of an aborted baby. We had a policy of not showing those, so we made an exception to our policy and had to scramble to find one and send it to them. The father's main concern was if the mom would be able to conceive again. She looked very numb during counseling. The advocate dug up some spiritual information about abortion being bad karma, but the dad was not willing to parent a child who was not typical[6]. They proceeded to have the abortion, which furthered our decision not to show graphic

---

6 Health is a very vague term. A Downes baby is not unhealthy, it is just a baby that is not typical. We've been told by Downes parents that this is the term they prefer.

pictures. If the dignity of the child cannot be respected by an ultrasound, then how can it be by showing the remains of an aborted child?

Why the Adoption Option Should Not be Forced

Our center was about three years old when a mother who had had an abortion, then married the father of the aborted baby, then had two more children came in with her daughter who was pregnant. The mother wanted her daughter to choose life, but she and the girl's father were in the process of getting a divorce. The mother of the client proposed adoption. She was planning to move out of state, and since her daughter had plans to go to college, she would take her daughter's baby with her. There was only one problem with that scenario. The daughter and she did not get along. The tension between the parents of the client was created by their first baby having been aborted. The house was filled with anger and pain, and the daughter's experience growing up was not one that made her want a child of her own to experience. The mother wanted her daughter to choose life, but she still drove her daughter to Planned Parenthood in support of her daughter's "choice." [7] She drove her twice—the first time she turned around and came back for more counseling. I remember seeing the twenty-week-old baby in the mother's womb from the outside. We prayed and hoped for the best, but the mother drove her daughter to Planned Parenthood again. The second time she did not leave with her baby.

A Dr. "Gosnell"[8] Client

A Bible school teacher walked into the abortion doctor's office and said, "I'll have the abortion if it's only one." After the abortion, the "doctor" said, "Congratulations, you just aborted twins." She came to

---

7 This is something that I have seen repeatedly with the parents' influence. If the parents are pro-life and supportive, the probability of the client choosing life is much greater than if the parents are pro-choice or pro-abortion.

8 Dr. Gosnell is an infamous doctor in Philadelphia who performed many heinous abortions. We're not sure of the exact doctor, but we gave him this fictitious name because of his callous treatment.

us hurting. She was in an abusive relationship. We helped her change the locks on her home. We had a nurse who had wanted to try to do some "post-abortive" counseling. The nurse had gone out for a course in the Midwest for a twelve-step program in post-abortive healing. She pulled out the manual from this course, which ended with instructing the post-abortive mother to forgive herself. This mother did just that. We thought we had "healed" her. She went back to her Bible school teaching job, and then two months later she checked herself into a psychiatric hospital under a suicide watch. We stopped doing post-abortive counseling after that.

The Prodigal Child

A very devout pro-life couple came to me with a situation with their daughter. There have been many pro-life families who have come to us for help with their children who are in crisis pregnancies. It is very challenging time for someone who is pro-life because it becomes personal. For the parents, it's not a time for second-guessing their parental skills. It's a time for action. That is why our approach is so successful. A discussion about where the baby will live and how their child's education will be completed is more calming than asking, "Why is this happening to us?" Certainly, better safeguards could have implemented, but sometimes the lessons for life are the most challenging and rewarding. In this case, the client chose life and had to navigate starting her career with a crisis pregnancy to consider, but her parents provided the needed support to make that transition workable. Several years later the client returned, and this time she felt remorse for her situation. She was worried about what her parents would think of her. I told her that they would be grateful for her to understand her actions now to make better choices in the future.

A Homeschooling Client

I homeschooled for nine years, and it was one of the biggest blessings in my life. I got to know my children and ground them in their faith, but sometimes it took every ounce of patience and self-sacrificing love that

I had. My husband would come home from work, and it was his time to be with the kids.

We had a client who was fourteen years old. Her mother was a single mom and worked at a fast-food place for over twelve hours a day. Her daughter became pregnant, and she decided that it was a good plan to homeschool because the public school had not protected her daughter from an unplanned pregnancy. We gave her an algebra tutor to work with her on her math skills and tried to get her connected to an online school. The challenge that single moms and dads face is to rely upon their children's school for teaching their kids about sexuality. Just as it was when I went to public school, it wasn't a question of when to become sexually active—it was a question of which birth control to use. Almost every client we have seen was using birth control before becoming pregnant. There is no substitute for supervision and always knowing where one's kids are.

The Late-Term Abortion Client
I was called into a rectory for a crisis case. The mom and dad just got the results from genetic testing. She was crying profusely. I tried to counsel her from a logical and emotional perspective, but I was very disturbed, because she was not being told that abortion was a mortal sin. I didn't think it was my place to do that. The priest just said, "Jesus loves you." Yes, most certainly, Jesus loves everyone, but He gives us free will to choose life or death. When we choose life, we are choosing God and happiness. When we choose death, we are choosing sadness and despair. I did refer her to mothers who has been in her situation and chose life, but I don't believe that was ultimately her decision.

A Moving-Out-of-Crisis Client
The most rewarding part of being the founder of an organization is to see clients who have moved on from their crisis pregnancy. I have seen former clients in my children's ballet classes, at their sporting events, but the best was the one who became my children's nurse. She had insurmountable odds. She was sleeping in an apartment where there were

bedbugs. She had to move everything out of her apartment while studying for her classes and taking care of two kids. She came for our free services, which helped her family in working her way through nursing school. She was balancing it all and getting good grades on top of everything that moms do. I had lost track of her until one day when my daughter needed some help. I walked into the pediatrician's office and there she was—enjoying the children who were with her through her crisis to her victory of becoming a nurse.

Creating Our Core Services of Saving Lives and Souls—Pregnancy Counseling, Parenting/Prenatal Classes

Our mission and charter outlined the framework of how we wanted to help, but it took time to learn and develop our own brand of helping. We wanted to work to change the lifestyle that created a crisis pregnancy, so just giving baby items away didn't seem to be the way to instruct our clients on the change of lifestyle. We needed the time to work with them, but our first approach at working with clients was limited to just giving things away. We had to create services to be able to have that time. Since the services we offered were free, this required a "currency" for coming to our centers. I reached out to Sister Nora from CORA[9], who described a system called the Baby Store. Clients could earn baby dollars by attending services. As soon as we had a Baby Store, we had clients coming for help so that we could work with them in moving out of crisis. The first parenting classes were an experiment. I tried to teach fast ways to cook healthy dinners. A volunteer demonstrated how to use a pressure cooker. Even though some of the clients were still bringing their fast food into the classes, it felt like the right thing to be doing—to inspire a healthier way to live. Some of the other topics that we were presenting were completely foreign to our clients: chastity, natural family planning, budgeting. We talked about not using birth control, and one of the clients blurted out "You expect my fourteen-year-old niece who is sexually active not to use anything?" We replied, "We expect your fourteen-year-old niece not to be sexually active." At the end of the year, we had a

---

9 www.coraservices.org

survey that asked which class taught them the most, and ironically, the woman who shouted out about her niece said it was the Chastity class because she "didn't want her boys to be dogs." We had to develop our own training methods that would work for a variety of skill bases, educational backgrounds, and natural gifts.

In order to save lives, our ability to show the developing baby was limited to fetal models. The models were anatomically correct and the right size and weight of a developing child. I remember one crisis mom holding one in her hands and shaking back and forth like the decision was in the palm of her hands. Sister Paula[10] had many good tips in her videos, like trying to relate to the client's reasons for considering abortion. What we did was to create a way to objectively approach the word "crisis." Why was this pregnancy a crisis? Was there enough food to eat? Were there educational goals to be met? By establishing goals in a crisis pregnancy, the client could see the light at the end of the tunnel. The advocates, who may or may not have experience with a crisis pregnancy, could draw on the experiences of their own crises by helping a client to organize her plan to get out of her crisis pregnancy.

Our prenatal classes had begun through our registered nurse, D.B. She initially would be called individually for each client, but as our client base grew, we started offering the prenatal classes as a group. D.B developed a presentation which showed the connection between birth control and abortion techniques. Since many birth control methods are abortifacients, the connection is very real. It is the lifestyle of promiscuity that creates most of our crisis pregnancies. It was very helpful to have a medical person share the education of a developing baby in a pro-life manner because our methods of helping are not limited to just saving lives.

We had a trained counselor come in from the beginning to help, and she was instrumental in helping to get the basic documentation needed. She taught us about the importance of an intake form, case notes, the concept of privacy, and how to work with clients. She helped me to understand setting an emotional boundary to protect myself and our clients from becoming too emotionally attached. This was an important

---

10 Sister Paula – Founder of International Life Services (www.internationallifeservices.org)

lesson for me to learn because as I started to work with clients, it was very difficult for me to not be drawn into their crises. One client, who was twenty-one years old, was about to have all her teeth removed. She had a condition that I never heard of in which all her teeth had be removed to alleviate tremendous pain. She was so young to be going through so much, including her crisis pregnancy. She lived on a street where there was open prostitution, so she couldn't just open her doors and let her kids play outside like my kids did at home. She was all alone, parenting a child in a bad neighborhood, and having all her teeth removed.

The boundary-setting was also good in the formation of our services. We were a self-help organization, meaning that the clients determined the length of time they needed us. They defined their goals as their boundary of service. Some of the volunteers, including the one who had been a part of our first save, had trouble maintaining the boundaries. She would take bagfuls of donations over to the client and would interrupt a party at the client's home. The initiative it takes for a client to get organized and show up at an appointment is the responsibility needed to care for a child. The client who may have issues with transportation, mobility issues, or financial issues must figure out all those moving parts to parent her child(ren) and get herself out of crisis.

Training Advocates

I was not a trained social worker, so I first tried to learn what other organizations did to train their workers. At the first training we had thirty-two people come. By the time the first crisis client came, there was only one advocate, an administrative person, and myself to take care of any clients. We had to learn a new system to train volunteers.

The second approach was to try a twelve-week program to cover all the concepts that an advocate should know. We found that after twelve weeks, we didn't have anyone left. Then we found Sister Paula and her International Life Services training videos. Sister Paula was a personal mentor for me and our centers, but her training videos are timeless, and seventeen years later, we still use them. We prescribe a schedule of about six sessions. The videos are watched, and volunteers are tested not for their expertise in counseling, but for their ability to come to the center and finish the training. If they do, afterward, we go over the procedures of that center and train them on our specific way of working with clients.

Some were skilled at working with the clients who were abortion-minded. Some were gifted at helping people learn the basics of counseling. What I had to offer was my educational background in systems engineering. I applied that technical expertise to developing a system that could be taught to other untrained people like me. We had the process down pat by the time we split into two centers. Clients would complete a Baby Store brochure with their goals. An advocate would work with the clients on how to find the resources needed and report the services delivered manually. By the time we had three centers, we were looking for ways to make our system more manageable and trainable and we had the opportunity when a database developer who had come to our center to fix our computers offered a website database. I could characterize our approach to helping our clients in the form of a website database. Clients' baby dollars could get automatically added/subtracted every time they attended their services or used them to purchase items. The clients' goals could be tracked, along with who their advocate was and how many times their services were attended—everything was available for anyone with computer skills. It was a game changer in terms of training. In the beginning, I had to learn other people's systems to be able to develop our own. I felt like ours did a better job at looking at a client's entire situation and was not just about the client choosing life.

Once we had three centers, it was time to find new leadership. I had been working in all aspects of the leadership for five years, and I was starting to fry. Initially, I would just elevate a volunteer to a leadership position and he/she would either work out or not. Some would leave because they felt that their authority was being challenged or not being respected, but most left because they weren't properly trained. It was time to develop a leadership course.

Leadership—Keeping the Mission at Heart

A spiritual advisor abruptly discharged himself as my advisor because he said I wasn't a good leader. As hurtful as this was in a personal assignation, I had to own what he was saying. I was not a strong leader. Anyone with a strong disposition about wanting things their way does not work in a morally bounded organization. I had to endure many inconveniences along the way to allow A Baby's Breath to be born. My family sometimes did not come first. The amenities sometimes were not according to my will. Certain individuals seized upon my good nature, thinking that they could take advantage of it. I usually accommodated requests and things not happening according to my way in lieu of the mission to help a mother to see her child take his/her first breath.

This was not an easy thing to teach other potential leaders who had been used to a structure wherein their decision was supreme. I had to step in when the leader's decision was ridiculous. For example, one leader decided that we should impose a requirement on our landlord to raise our dropped ceilings six inches. I would not back that decision, and so she left. She completely disregarded the project at hand—which was to move our center two stories up—and left because of her dismissed request. As a result, I had to manage two centers at once. We were starting another center at the time, so my time was limited. I was unloading about two hundred messages left on the answering machine a couple of weeks after she left. By the time I got to an abortion-minded client, she had already aborted. It was another example of leadership that needed to be focused on the mission and not so much on the peripheral issues.

Leadership Course—Teaching Our Way

My job for the first five years of A Baby's Breath's existence was to take care of all aspects of leadership. I was the executive director, the president, and the one keeping track of most of the data for clients, volunteers, and donors. I was near the breaking point when I started writing my jobs down and organizing them into categories. I had one for people (director jobs), one for money matters (general manager jobs), and one for computer inputting (donation coordinator jobs). I found that creating these lists was critical because it created a boundary of responsibility so that there would be no stepping on toes among the leadership positions. A volunteer leader could pick which area he/she felt comfortable in and take on only that leadership position. The advantage of our system is that no leader can assume power over/monopolize the center or organization with his or her own personal agenda. Also, the organization would not burden one person with many roles, as many social service organizations do to their executive directors.

Many leadership courses are set up to motivate their leaders for more success in their efforts to advance their organization. Our leadership course is a one-day, once-a-year opportunity to regenerate, rejuvenate, and start centers. We structured the course to teach the three different types of leaders at A Baby's Breath—the director, the general manager and the donations coordinator. Each of the three types of leaders were trained so that, if needed, they could individually administer a crisis center.

Leadership—Overcoming Bullies

Bullies sometimes don't come with warning labels. Sometimes they are very unassuming, and one thinks they will just accommodate their position with grace. Other times they will get entrenched by taking all aspects of responsibility and then twisting the system until their way is recognized. When starting a center, we were especially prone to attracting this type of leadership. It's a challenge when starting a center to have the dominant leaders not take over the operation. One leader that we had installed was herself in a crisis pregnancy. She had self-control issues, but she had a very good heart. We elevated her to the position of leader in the absence of anyone else who wished to take the responsibility. She was extremely good at working with clients to get them set up on welfare and at hearing their problems. She was loving and gave the clients the needed compassion in their lives. Our system, however, is self-help-based. It requires discipline to teach our clients how to get out of crisis. It's like mother or father who sometimes must teach tough love for the children to learn how to survive in this world. The leader herself needed structure. We ultimately had to dismiss her because of her lack of organization and not showing up for her shifts.

Other leaders have shown too much authority over our clients and not enough heart. Screaming and getting upset with clients is never acceptable, even if the client is not doing her best at getting herself organized and motivated to get out of a crisis. Our approach is to allow the client to articulate what needs to get done in his/her life to move through the crisis. If the client can identify the goals, he or she is more likely to own the goals personally.

We have had leaders who think they can change our system to their own, even after seeing the success of an operational center. One leader decided he didn't like to use our form of advertising and refused to be the leader if we chose to do that form of advertising. We had already sold that advertisement in our sponsorship letter and so we were obligated to use it, leaving us stuck between the will of the leader and our contractual obligations to our sponsors. We had to lose that leader to accommodate our sponsors' paid advertising. It was sad because he was so committed to the perfection of his service that he lost sight of the goal to finance the cause for life.

The times when bad leaders are replaced are especially tenuous. The leader's legacy could be rippled in the defection of volunteers who feel a loyalty to that leader over the mission of the organization. That is why our system is so helpful. Our centers can operate without one of the leadership positions being filled. We can continue our services if we have advocates to serve clients and the financial ability to pay our bills.

Finding the "Perfect Director"

It took eleven years to find her, but she finally came. Kate Chetta took over in 2011 after the previous director decided it was time to move on. She prayed before accepting. She is highly organized, very affable, and provides structure and guidance to volunteers and clients. She is the standard by which we can judge our future directors. She balances her busy family life with that of the center. It's not an easy job to fill, and not an easy path to take with family, but from my experience it is the path that God needed me to take, and hopefully Kate will have the same blessing that I have experienced.

A Natural Way to Plan Family—Service

Mike and Lisann Castagno have been practitioners and providers of natural family planning (NFP) classes for years. Their life mirrors the teachings of the Catholic catechism, which is to respect each other's bodies for their intended purposes. They have sacrificed their time in teaching others. We have started to offer free classes in the sympto-thermal method. Initially, the plan was to use only couples who practiced this method, but the pool of couples who used NFP to regulate their pregnancies and are willing to share their time is limited. We are now trying to implement a training program for instructors who have a medical background and who can teach the method. There are other forms of NFP to include such as NAPRO and the Billings Method, but these methods require highly educated professionals, and our free volunteer structure does not support offering this type of NFP. All methods of NFP require communication, which is key in any good marriage.

The Path to Peace—Blessings of Sacrifice

When I was in the middle of handling all the leadership positions, I used to dream about having partners that helped me to balance my life with the administration of the organization. It is so rewarding to see that the center that was first started when I was homeschooling two kids and expecting my fourth thriving as my kids are now graduating high school and college and beginning their own lives. Creating A Baby's Breath has not been a detriment to my family's well-being—quite the opposite. My daughter (cofounder of A Baby's Breath) witnessed her first prayer vigil at an abortion clinic recently and saw the importance of the work that Mom has done over the past seventeen years. She now understands why Mom didn't go back to work to make it financially easier for our family. She loves her brothers and can enjoy their love, the way that our clients who have been supported in their choices for life can love their families.

KAREN JANE PATOTA, FOUNDER

Figure 7- Co-Founder of A Baby's Breath

Figure 8- A Baby's Breath - Jeffersonville - beautiful sign of hope

Creating Our Second Center in Collegeville

We were invited into Collegeville by Monsignor Patrick Sweeney. He was considering our organization's model for a crisis pregnancy center along with another and chose ours. He liked our holistic approach to helping everyone in a crisis pregnancy, including the family that needed support beyond the choice. He wanted to use our center as a focus of his parish's pro-life efforts in his community. We were very honored to accommodate his wishes. We were going to manage the center, and he would provide the financial and volunteer support in getting the center off the ground.

The first decision that we made was that we didn't think our Baby Store would be needed in a more affluent community and college town, but that turned out to be a key way to get our services attended, just like in Jeffersonville. Our space in Collegeville was quite a bit smaller than that in Jeffersonville, so we had to manage with fewer items in the Baby Store. The parenting classes, prenatal classes, and pregnancy counseling services were all fully functional within a year of starting the center. This was the advantage of having a set formula in place at the time of opening the second center.

Planned Parenthood's Neighbor

In looking for a space to rent, the director at the time found one right in Planned Parenthood (PP)'s building. We didn't know what to expect. Were there going to be confrontations between the workers? We opened our doors on August 15, 2005, with a Mass, and it seemed to bring the light of Truth into the building. From that point forward, we conducted our business in the way we always have: with a positive and welcoming spirit. We took our brochures into the PP center, and they started referring clients to us who were choosing life. It was, however, difficult to learn about the clients who we tried to help who had gone to PP for their RU486. The clients would go back to their dorms and deliver their children in the dorm bathrooms. The PP in our building closed its doors in 2011 by the grace of God. The prayer warriors who stood and prayed faithfully on the sidewalk outside until PP's closing could move onto other abortion clinics and hospitals, but we stayed to help the mothers, fathers, and families who were in crisis pregnancies.

The Angel Club—A New Way to Donate
In starting a new center, we had to consider another way of raising funds because all of the current fund-raisers were dedicated toward existing expenses. John J. Giorgis, who became the general manager of our Collegeville center, proposed a way for donors to give to our center by a monthly subscription program. He intended to get the parish involved in our Angel Club program, but it was not accepted by the parish, so we had to start from scratch in building our Angel Club program. While we had a minimal number of subscribers initially, the program has grown substantially to now support all of our centers. When our database was updated, we were able to have the Angel Club donations come through our website, and now approximately 25 percent of all our centers' budgets is from the Angel Club program.

A New Way to Defend Life
In 2009, the Knights of Columbus wanted to donate an ultrasound machine. David Corrozza, PhD. was the one who proposed this to us, and I proposed in return that he become our general manager. He generously accepted and we proceeded to figure out how to offer free ultrasounds to our abortion-minded clients. We were a nonmedical center and organization, so this involved learning the needed positions to deliver a

"medical" service. We had to find a medical director, ultrasound nurse, and ultrasound technicians. All of these positions had to be volunteers for our medical malpractice insurance.

We were guided by Dr. Lester Ruppersberger, who was the medical director at Bucks County Women's Center. He helped us to understand the configuration necessary to conduct low-level ultrasounds to detect heartbeats, calculate gestational age, and confirm an intrauterine pregnancy. We needed a medical director to offer up his medical license for our malpractice insurance, a radiologist to interpret the scan, a RN to be our ultrasound nurse, and ultrasound technicians. We found Dr. Daniel D. Beninati, a retired OB-GYN who was devoted to life and wanted to help our mission. Dr. James offered to be our radiologist. Susan McInerney, RN, offered to be our ultrasound nurse. Our first ultrasound technicians was Brandy.

We worked for eighteen months on the procedures, and then we finally offered our first scan. The client on whom it was performed was already choosing life, but it was nonetheless miraculous to have this capability and gift to defend life. It's since been very instrumental in saving lives.

Finding Mom

There have been so many wonderful volunteers at this center, and so many blessings, but it didn't start out that way. The first director, who was so helpful in finding our space, quit in the first month. This left a void for me to fill until we found a permanent volunteer director. She was the one at church who checked off all the boxes when we distributed the volunteer cards. She had to train herself with the advocate training, but she was patient, kind, and strong all at the same time. I used to go to her when running the centers was the most challenging. She had the most nonjudgmental disposition of anyone I had met through the years. It was like finding a mom in Mary Ann McDonnell, director of Collegeville for six years.

One of the advocates at Collegeville, Maryann Gullick, was the "oldest" advocate we have at A Baby's Breath. She was at Jeffersonville when we first started. I learned how to be a director and manager from Maryann. She would do everything that I had asked her to do with grace.

She, too, was an amazing, patient person for our clients, just as many of our volunteers are. She could relate to situations with our clients and help them emotionally navigate a difficult time.

Overcoming Adversity—Finding the Silver Lining

The director quit in the first month and she didn't just quit—she locked up our system and sent a virus to my home computer. We had to bring in an outfit that would unlock our system and pay $5,000 for that to be done. The silver lining was finding Mark Hitchcock, our gifted website database designer and developer. He proposed a database that was more flexible and user-friendly so that our novice social workers and computer people could keep track of baby dollars and services in the same place our volunteer/donor/resources were kept. He generously donated storing our website and website database with unlimited storage capability. Mark could create modules for keeping track of our Run for Life information and incorporate the ability for our website to take donations for our Angel Club. Mark saved us close to $20,000 in not having to buy licenses for our silent auction software. He's been a Godsend to our organization. He's been on call for maintenance for the past eleven years with very minimal compensation. We would not have the five centers and the home if we didn't have Mark. God always has a plan, and if we trust in Him, He will provide.

Overcoming the Competition

Our center was the chosen place for our church sponsor, and yet on the church property was a sign that directed crisis clients to call to an office located twenty-five miles away. We have seen this kind of idiocy repeatedly. Why didn't the sign have the number of our center, which was in the same community? The fiefdoms that exist in the pro-life world are beyond understanding. Certainly, a center that provides confidential counseling has volunteer requirements and methods they must follow. If a volunteer does not fit into the requirements or will not abide by the mission and charter, there should be alternatives for a pro-life person to actively participate. But for the most part, the divisions are personal and do not consider the higher priority of saving lives and souls.

Homosexual Crisis Clients

This wasn't our first crisis couple, and it wasn't our only homosexual couple, but it still impressed me as a true crisis in the case where one of the partners was pregnant. A crisis pregnancy is the living proof of infidelity, which was the case in this situation. One of the partners was in a relationship with her son's friend. It was challenging in not knowing which angle to hit, but the priority was for the mom to choose life. We got advisement from our spiritual director on how to handle these difficult cases, but it was nonetheless frustrating to see a more dominant partner with a more young and vulnerable partner. The truth of their relationship was evident in the crisis pregnancy. Clearly, a straight-up chastity discussion would never work in trying to help this client not return in another crisis pregnancy.

A "Memorable" Memorial Day

We'd had our ultrasound functioning for nine months when the call came through the center cell regarding a young man who wanted to save his baby. This was not his first crisis, and it was the second time the mom was not choosing life. She acquiesced to letting him see his baby on the ultrasound. I stood next to him as he saw his child dancing on the ultrasound screen. I looked at her and at first I thought there were tears of joy in her eyes. I looked again and saw the glee of a dog about to pounce on its victim. I tried to talk to her privately, and her spirit seemed to be tormented. She would ask me if I thought she was a bad person, and I said that the abortion decision would be bad. No amount of logical discussion could convince her to choose life—she would not allow a six-month baby his or her first breath. Abortion was the only choice that she would consider.

Our Committed Cell Phone Holder

We had a need for someone to hold the cell phone in 2012 when we established our ultrasound service. What we found was an angel in waiting, Susan McInerney, RN. She is always ready with a compassionate sweet voice to take the calls of our crisis clients. She even takes the phone on

CREATING COMPASSIONATE PLACES

vacation with her. Sometimes she is met with gratitude, and sometimes she is not. Her devotion in offering the lifeline of support goes toward helping our crisis clients see their children on the ultrasound screen and with being an advocate for navigating through the clients' crises. It's been her joy and our blessing to have her witness the choices of life and beyond through the service of our ultrasound.

Uncommon Valor

The most inspiring volunteers that I have seen over the past seventeen years have been the volunteers who are in crisis themselves and yet give of their time. Susan Grant, our director for the past five years, came to us after getting downsized. She continued to work with us after finding her permanent job because she could relate to the need for our center and what we provide. She is a role model for our clients, many of whom are choosing poverty in choosing life. Our clients are treated with respect and dignity in the same way that we wish to be treated. The strength of the organization has been through the unrecognized charity and support we give freely to our clients.

Figure 9- A Baby's Breath - Collegeville - with the former neighbors, Planned Parenthood

Creating Our Third Center on the Main Line

Why the Main Line Area?—Saint David's Center

The question was asked many times: Why start a center on the Main Line? The answer was that there was a need for what we do here. There were so many colleges near Planned Parenthood (PP) in St. David's (Main Line). PP picks the areas where there is a need for crisis pregnancy intervention. We chose the location of our first center on the Main Line to be less than half a block away from the abortion providing PP. While we were grateful for the opportunity to serve the community, the community was not so receptive to us. We didn't realize how many churchgoing people supported the right to an abortion or access to contraception. Our mission was not to last in Saint David's, however. The landlord jacked up our rent 25 percent, and we had to find a different location from which to operate.

The Bryn Mawr Experience

The new leaders found a location that was located directly across from the movie theater. The landlord's name was Jude, and the leader saw a stained-glass window with Simon and Jude, so the leader thought this was a sign that we needed to make our new Main Line center in a space that cost $24,000 per year. While it did have a good location, one would have to come to a complete stop on a busy road and look up to the second floor to see our center. The stairs leading up to the space were very narrow. Still, the space looked fresh and inviting, so we decided to give the leaders the benefit of the doubt and go with the most expensive location we had ever rented. This was a painful lesson to learn, that ownership of contractual obligations is not readily accepted. What I have done over the past seventeen years is say yes to the bills from which many volunteers and leaders have simply walked away. Picking up the pieces of many disenfranchised, disillusioned volunteers has been the way that all the centers have survived.

The Pain of the Post-Abortive Volunteer

As soon as we moved into our beautiful new space in Bryn Mawr, I received a call from a potential volunteer. She had read our website which included the testimony about my inspiration coming from a post abortive friend and was very eager to help. She gave her own story of being a post-abortive mother. She was the daughter of a midwife and had found herself pregnant. Her first instinct was to abort, but she turned around in the first visit. She prayed and went back and had the abortion. She then married the dad, and they had more children, but she couldn't forgive herself. She went to a therapist and she said there were many clients that she saw who were in the same position of hurting after their abortions. She told the therapist about a recurring dream of seeing the baby and the abortion doctor, and told her husband she thought about joining the aborted baby. She didn't stay on as a volunteer. We've had a couple of post-abortive women and men come to help, but most end up leaving for one reason or another. I'm just assuming the pain of seeing women with their children is too difficult for them.

Teaching Our Way of Fund-Raising

Teaching the concept of what we do to people who have never used their professional expertise in a volunteer capacity is not easy. Our methods are simple, but they have effectively helped thousands of clients. Our Run for Life has been the primary vehicle for keeping the doors of our first center open for almost twenty years. The simplicity of just one fundraiser supporting the center for the next calendar year is sometimes a challenge for people to understand. The concept of sponsorship instead of constant fund-raising is sometimes impossible to teach. The budget of our new center was $24,000, so the fund-raising had to match it. One of the leaders suggested that we hold an ice cream fund-raiser. This probably would have been an ideal fund-raiser for a pro-life group at church but for the center with recurring bills and contracts to meet, this was not a good plan. The leader was optimistically thinking that we could achieve a $5,000 goal by the participants in the fund-raiser downloading a coupon, going to an ice cream shop on one day, and buying enough ice cream to raise $5,000. This would mean that $50,000 in ice cream would need to be sold in one day. My guess is that the shop doesn't sell that much ice cream for the whole year, so the probability was that the return would never be realized. My math skills were critical in articulating the impossibility of this fund-raiser.

Free Professional Help

I never considered myself a professional social worker, so there were no barriers or obstacles to overcome in providing free help to our clients. I didn't have the letters behind my name, and most of our workers don't either, but the number-one qualification for helping at A Baby's Breath is to care about people who are in a crisis pregnancy. One leader wanted our parenting classes to have a professional parenting class instructor. She researched and found a person who was highly trained in "single parenting." Her fee was $350 per class. It was then my seventh year of working with single parents, and what we had done to form our parenting classes was to build a list of people with letters behind their names who would come and instruct for free. I really didn't have an agenda in building that list. It was who was available that determined the order. I didn't have a complete idea at the beginning of the year who we would have as clients, but I just wanted our single parents to have a place to come once a month and be a part of a group of other single parents. Many of the single parents that we helped in our first location were stereotypical welfare clients. I had seen the transformation in their demeanor and self-esteem just by being with people who talked to them respectfully. What we were trying to teach our clients was how to create a community of love and support for one another. The main thing that

I learned from starting a center in an area of affluence is that services of value are not done for free. The fact that we had no money in the budget for paid professionals was secondary to the desire for perfection.

Sometimes There Is a Need for Professionals

We had a crisis cell phone that was held by me exclusively for the first five years. Sometimes, early on, I would sleep with it next to my bed. I would intercept the desperate phone calls of crisis clients. Crisis moms and dads would have me at their beck and call 24/7. I began to share the phone to allow volunteers to be trained up on how to answer client phone calls. Just as I was never trained how to be an "expert" crisis counselor, I baptized new volunteers with their first call by handing them a crisis cell phone. One new director who had never been pregnant and had never heard of an ectopic pregnancy had a crisis call from a mom who had gone to Planned Parenthood (PP). PP told her she had an ectopic pregnancy and should go to the hospital to get the abortion pill. The director called me and tried to help a client who wanted to choose life. I was familiar with the term "ectopic" as I was a mother and knew about the complications of pregnancy. I knew that someone who had an ectopic pregnancy could not choose life and would have to have a tube removed if in fact the embryo was in the fallopian tubes[11], as is the case with an ectopic pregnancy. It didn't make sense that PP would give the diagnosis of an ectopic pregnancy without checking the hormonal levels to confirm. Within a week, we had three phones calls with the same situation and we discovered a method that PP was using to have clients get the abortion pill delivered through the local Catholic hospital, which gave the abortion pill only in instances of an ectopic pregnancy. We realized at that point that the phone should be held by a medically trained person so that the proper questions could be asked. Our attorney wrote a letter to the Catholic hospital to inform them of PP's way of circumventing a pro-life hospital policy.

---

11 Having a Fallopian tube removed is not an abortion. Abortion by definition in the Catholic Catechism is a direct and willful act. It is not directly killing an unborn baby to have the Fallopian tube removed and if the Fallopian tube is not removed could in fact kill the mother.

A Good Professional

Joanna McGrath, CNM, WHNP, was one of the good professionals we had come to our Main Line center. She didn't try to change our system, but instead strove to learn it. She helped us with supervising interns, organizing the leadership course, and being the face of the pro-life medical professional. Her contributions live on in a help center on the Main Line in the form of qualified, medically trained personnel coming to our fold to help with our mission.

Fund-Raiser Naming Should Contain the Name of the Organization

This lesson was learned early in the start of A Baby's Breath when it was proposed that the proceeds should go in part toward the family who had lost a loved one. The eighth grader was a parishioner, and the Run for Life committee thought this would be a great way to pay homage to the loved one and his/her family. We agreed that our funds were best used by going toward the solution to abortion, like the proceeds of all our fund-raisers. We were in that situation again when a fund-raiser for the Main Line center was proposed to partner with a family who lost someone. Their only stipulation was that we change the name of our fund-raiser. We were in a tough spot, so we acquiesced. Even though the fund-raiser was an enormous financial success initially, the name of our organization was not propagated with the execution of the fund-raiser. Ultimately, it was decided to separate our causes in order to make decisions that were best for advertising our center and organization's mission. Our organization's name was the name of the place where mothers, fathers, and families needed to come to save lives.

Surviving Changes in Leadership, Competition and another Planned Parenthood closing

With any organization or business, challenges lie in recreating itself through dramatic changes. This was especially the case in our Main Line center. No other center has had to deal with this level of volatility of leadership. We have had interns from Villanova University to manage while we continued our search. Several other leaders came and went because, for one reason or another, they decided their time was better spent elsewhere. One starts to question whether the journey is worth it with so many pitfalls. One former social worker named Nicole came to help us bridge the gap over from our location in Bryn Mawr to a new one in Wayne, where our rent would be reduced to a third of the old rent. Our space was also reduced to only 450 square feet, but we were in the heart of the Main Line and again within one mile of Planned Parenthood. Nicole worked diligently to rebuild the volunteer leadership at Wayne. The reward was when we saw PP close its doors. It was a special day to see the closing of an institution that preys upon young women to facilitate a lifestyle that creates crisis pregnancies. We were then the only center on the Main Line set up to help mothers, fathers, and families in crisis pregnancies, but that didn't stop the pro-life competition from trying to redirect clients and volunteers to centers far away.

Finding a Perfect Director for Wayne

Brittany Sedlak was the most successful director in the history of A Baby's Breath's Main Line centers. She had counseling experience and a natural ability to pick up the A Baby's Breath system. Nicole had spotted her talents and immediately trained her to the position. She was kind and gentle in all her ways. This came into play when dealing with a woman who was raped and choosing life. She allowed the mother to vent her frustrations and humiliations with her situation. This is the way that most of our counseling works, but Brittany offered the spiritual aspect that is unique to our help centers. It is only through the grace of God that our clients are choosing life. For both the untrained and trained, our system works by giving options, resources, prayer, and time that allow a mother to choose life. Brittany was also the women's coordinator of our Loving our Life service. She provided the private time needed for single women who were choosing a Christian lifestyle. Her tenure at A Baby's Breath ended when she got married and moved away, but it is our hope that it is a momentary pause in her leadership as she is hoping to start an A Baby's Breath center in Washington, DC.

The Loving our Life Service

Teaching others how to live a Christian lifestyle can be challenging in a culture where the Christian moral standard is not applied, recognized, or even accepted. God intended Christians to live separately and chastely until married. Of course, A Baby's Breath offers help to mothers and fathers who find themselves pregnant. The plan is to offer support for those who are single— whether they are in a relationship or not—because choosing chastity becomes more challenging when there is a significant other to consider. Choosing the right dress code, environment, prayer life, and company are important contributions to a lifestyle that is consistent with Christ. Pete Rawson is the coordinator of the Men's Loving our Life service, and his life replicates what we should ascribe in our life. His life was met with unforeseen challenges, and his response was not of rejection to God's plan, but to embrace it with grace. He lives the life of devotion to serving God and others in a crisis pregnancy as our Jeffersonville general manager and to help others not to be in a crisis pregnancy in his work with Loving our Life. His life is one and the same with the Gospel teaching.

Post-Abortive support

The need to continues to support post-abortive mothers and fathers who come in with another crisis pregnancy. A crisis mother was crying profusely and demonstrating the classic signs of depression. Our first goal was to seek help for her depression. We referred her to a priest for Confession, as she was a Catholic. After that, she needed more support for her past abortion decision, but we are not the professionals that are needed for this kind of help. Once the client was affirmatively choosing life for herself and her baby, our mission was complete. Post-abortive parents have the loudest voice in terms of verbalizing the hurt that they feel from their abortions. It is only through their experience that the horror of legalized abortion can be ended.

Figure 10 - A Baby's Breath - Wayne's sign shared with the Loving our Life sign

CREATING OUR FOURTH CENTER IN WARMINSTER

Finding a Founder

We began our leadership course in 2009. In 2010, a woman came from a law practice to learn about leadership. When she left, she was inspired to start a center in Warminster. The homework was to assemble a team of four—just like we had started with in our first center. The location was to be as close as possible to the Warminster Planned Parenthood. The woman was a businesswoman and she was pro-life. It wasn't until years later that it was revealed that she really hadn't intended on starting a center, but after coming to our course was so inspired. She was a good student and had her team ready to start fund-raising for their first center. They held their first Run for Life at the Tyson State Park in Ridesboro. It raised enough money for an entire year's rent. She surveyed the new location, and while it didn't have all the recommended features, like two entrances, it was in the same business complex as Planned Parenthood, which performed twenty surgical abortions a week at that location. In 2011, on behalf of A Baby's Breath, she locked into a four-year lease, and we were underway for saving lives and souls in Warminster.

Interruption—The Pro-Life Competition

Two months before the second fund-raiser, the local board decided to propose changing the name of our Warminster center. They had read on a national pro-life leader's website that people were not to take abortion-minded clients to centers with the word "baby" in their name. While this was going on, my husband was having major surgery, and my attention was less focused on the name of the organization than it was on my husband's health. We were also planning a family vacation. I quickly organized a teleconference to discuss the prospect of changing our name. The founder requested to have this meeting in person. The corporate board's decision was to keep our name the same. We had saved lives with the word "baby" in it, so the board didn't understand the group's decision to take the word out of it.

On top of that, one of the group's volunteers had found out that we were going to do a singles support group with a yoga class. Someone from their group called one of our biggest sponsors and told him we weren't real Catholics, and he called me to discuss that in terms of his support. We canceled the yoga class and went in a different direction for ideas of supporting singles.[12]

With the corporate board's decision, the group met and decided to abort their plans to participate in a center at Warminster. My partner J.B. had gone to the meeting to represent the corporate board's decision of not changing the name, and he was accused of not being pro-life or caring about babies. Scripture was quoted about why he wasn't pro-life, and the bottom line was that all but one of the group's members left—two months before the second annual fund-raiser.

I'm sure no one who left thought about the impact of leaving the organization they way that I did. As president of an organization for the past seventeen years, I have seen people leave without notice, without trying to find a replacement, for reasons that are their own, and not for the reasons they had begun working with us—to help save lives and souls.

A New Beginning

Enter Saint Maryanne Thompson, a nonprofit owner who offered to help me reconstruct the group that would be the new Warminster

---

12 It is noted that some Catholic organizations decry yoga as a form of exercise. The point that is being made is the tact of a volunteer to contact one of our donors directly. One cannot prepare oneself well enough for volunteers who have ill intentions.

board. She identified the perfect people to fill the open positions. She picked an excellent director and a new general manager, Anne Ruegner. She helped to organize the Run for life and assemble the needed parts to be able to function as we typically do. It was a very big blessing to have Maryanne resurrect our center. She applied her professional talents to help us to be able to save lives and souls in Warminster.

Lifesaving Work

A Knights of Columbus group offered to provide an ultrasound to our Warminster center. The Collegeville center already had one, but we accepted the offer, given our proximity to Planned Parenthood. It took a while to get the center ready to do the medical procedure, but we were ready for doing ultrasounds just in time for a lifesaving intervention. The director spotted a couple in the parking lot looking desperate. She found out from them that their reason for being there was to have an abortion at Planned Parenthood that morning. She asked them if they wanted to see their baby on the ultrasound. They said yes. They had many reasons for why they were in a crisis pregnancy, but when they saw their baby, the only choice that mattered was to choose life.

Saving Lives with Our Name

The general manager had proposed an advertising campaign in 2014. It was our most expensive campaign to date. We had procured the abortion statistics from Google, and in the months of December to January, the abortion rate had spiked from 20 abortions to 150. We decided it was worth the investment to see if lives could be saved. One client who was considering an abortion called our center after driving past the sign. She had an ultrasound and chose life. She considered adoption until the very end, when the baby's beautiful face convinced her to parent the child. It was a disappointment to the mom who was going to be the adoptive mom, but nonetheless, life was chosen in a center with the word "baby" in the name.

The Rose Garden Service

Amy Brooks is a very affable and engaging mom. She was determined to find a sibling for her son who was adopted. She didn't just find one, she found two from a mother who generously chose to allow Amy and her husband the opportunity to parent twins. The Rose Garden is an online Facebook group offering emotional support, information on adoption, and a place where other couples waiting to adopt can share their journey.

Redirecting Clients

We were approached by an outfit who was proposing a different way to advertise to our clients. Their proposal was that we would pay them $1,000 per month and we would collect information and help the clients seeking help. We didn't know what we were paying for until we decided not to participate in their campaign. We then saw a drop in our crisis clients, and that was because they were not being directed toward our centers. Instead, clients from our zip codes would be directed to a center forty-five minutes away that was participating in the campaign.

We've never caved to competition pressure before, and it has not been to our detriment. Our advertising campaigns advertise what we do and how we do it. We wear our pro-life label on the front door and continue with that through all our services. It has been our way to attract new volunteers as well as new clients—the abortion-minded as well as those who just need help with their crisis pregnancies. We believe we're rebuilding the culture of life when we do this.

Figure 11- A Baby's Breath - Warminster advertising billboard

Creating our Fifth Center in Phoenixville—Our First Home

Offer for More Space

The Deacon from Saint Ann's parish called and asked me what we would do with five thousand square feet of space. I immediately said that we would use the space to offer emergency housing for our pregnant clients. It had been our experience that homeless pregnant people were not a high priority of other housing solutions. Every time we had a homeless pregnant client, we would scramble to find housing. Sometimes the solution was the couch of a friend; sometimes we would pay for a couple of nights in a hotel. We tried to place clients in some existing homeless shelters for mothers, but usually they were full and could not accommodate them. We didn't realize until starting our own home how difficult it is to offer housing. It was easier to raise the funds and transition into housing use than it was to start a housing service.

Using That Same Model for a Home

By the time we started the home, our organization was sixteen years old. We had operated with an all-volunteer leadership organization, giving stipends to a few workers, but none more than $5,000 annually. We thought we would evolve our home from this basic model. The home had to go through two transitions—one to transition from a day care to a counseling center (what we have at all the other centers), and the other to finally become a home. The first transition didn't require much money, just a ramp and a few minor fixes were needed, but the second transition was going to require $60,000 in renovation costs, including a sprinkler system, an egress from the third floor, and upgrades to our fire protection system. We had a Run for Life fund-raiser that covered most of the costs for the first transition, and then through a golf outing fund-raiser we covered the rest of the transition costs to become a home. We were legally ready for the business of offering housing, but not entirely ready for running a housing service. There were many new issues to deal with in terms of managing volunteers and clients 24/7 instead of the short span of time we had to do that in our other core services centers. We had many lessons to learn, but just as with starting the first center – we just trusted God that we would be successful in our efforts.

Finding a Good House Mom

On our first try, we hired a homeless person to be our first house mom. She seemed ideal in her qualifications, being a former social worker. We thought she would appreciate our beautiful accommodations, sharing her experience of being a mom, and that she would relate to the inhabitants' position of being homeless with compassion. We were sadly disappointed when she became embroiled in arguments with our clients. She would disobey the house rules and create issues with the house director. We didn't realize how difficult it would be to remove her as our house mom until we were finally forced into that situation. Rehoming a homeless person who hadn't worked for the past six years (except for us) and who didn't have sufficient credit proved to be a challenge. Finally, her family members picked her up, and we hope that she's in a better home now.

The pursuit of finding the next house mom started with a board member's family member. The board did not think she was a good candidate, but were not willing to be forthright with their contention. It is an awkward moment when the personnel decisions of a board become too personal. My recommendation is that house moms should not be too closely tied to any board members.

The board moved on to another candidate who was ideal. She had a degree in counseling, and the situation worked for both her and A

Baby's Breath. She was perfect for all of two months until she received "an offer too good to turn down." There is no guarantee in any one person, so the prospect of having someone last forever is not a reasonable assumption. The plan should always be to plan for change because that's what will give hope for the future of offering housing.

Other Departures

When the final transitions were made and we had a lease to be signed, I drew together everyone involved and mentioned that this was a four-year contract. Even though the lease was very attractive and affordable, I wanted the group to own the decision to open a home seriously. Everyone around the table nodded their heads like they understood, and yet from the time of the first meeting until now, only one person from the founding board is left to carry on the cross. It's not like I was surprised, just disappointed that they would not be able to take part in the victory of seeing our first clients carry their babies out of being homeless into a life that was independent and out of crisis.

Our First Success

She was homeless and pregnant and her children had been taken from her because she was homeless. Her family encouraged her to have an abortion. She chose life and came to live at the home. She was very respectful of our rules and appreciative of her gift of housing. Even during a tenuous time at the home, with a house mom who had issues and other clients who were problematic, this client was why we chose to bear the burden of offering housing. She is now in recovery and starting her life over again. She continues to come for our individual parenting classes, and we enjoy helping her as much as she enjoys coming back to us.

The Enjoyable Workers

I have said that my motivations for enduring seventeen years of sacrifice are the appreciative clients and the good volunteers. This is so true. There are many self-sacrificing workers here. Kim Granito, who started in our first center as a barn attic coordinator[13], stepped it up to become a corporate board member and housing volunteer. She was also the person who recommended our organization when the deacon from her parish was looking for an organization to transition a convent into useable space. She introduced us to many friends, including Janet Mancini and Penny Pavucek, who joined Karen Ferich, Rachael Jasienski, and Joanne Kusko to form the housing board and was devoted to providing a safe place to transition into a different life. It's not because it's easy, but because it's needed that volunteers have come to help at A Baby's Breath.

The Road to Independence

After the second successful golf outing, a group of businesspeople asked us what we would do with a large sum of money. We had finished the housing transition, so we decided we would apply the funds toward getting our clients out of crisis. Fred Cianni, director of the Independence program, is now helping our crisis clients to evaluate their resumes, create a budget, find jobs, and transition their lives out of crisis and off government support.

Our Good Leader

Joanne Kusko is an excellent role model for our clients. She is a tough lady, and I tell her that. She needed to be tough in her own life when her first husband left her with four children. She went back to school, got her degree, and then when her life became more stable after her second marriage, decided to give back and take on a leadership role at the church. She took a cut in salary to do so. Now she gets no compensation for the aggravation that she's had to endure in starting and running our home. She is a devout and holy person from whom our clients can learn much. We are so blessed to have her.

---

13 The barn attic coordinator had responsibility to organize and transport items to and from the storage place for baby items.

The Final Test of Our Model
We are hopeful that the low-budget way of offering free housing will work, but it relies upon the model of a shared leadership. We have established a housing board; however, it will be a challenge to balance the power of strong leadership needed to govern a home. For the sake of homeless pregnant moms, we embrace our challenge.

Book Three - How to Start New Centers/Services with the A Baby's Breath Model

Once one has a mission and a group of people willing to work toward the goal of one's organization, it's time to put the task to work. The A Baby's Breath model does not start with the expenses first. We start with the resources to manage a list of expenses. The very first A Baby's Breath center came from a Run for Life. We had $5,000, but our budget to manage the first year was about $8,000. We began to reach out to our friends from church, family friends, and friends of life, and once we had our income matching our expenses, we were prepared to open.

Keys to Development

1) **Find your first board.** The first board should include an initial director, general manager, and donations coordinator (if one has people willing to assume titles). Note: it has been my experience that initial key leaders do not always survive through the opening of a center. It takes a very bold person to say yes to an endeavor that is not seen. Sometimes, that personality will not meld well into a shared configuration once the center is established or there is a bit of transition time to be considered. If one cannot find people to take on titles, but instead have individuals who would be willing to do the work of a "director, general manager or donations coordinator" in an acting capacity – this might be advantageous because one might be able to see if the person fits the job or vice versa as the center opens.
2) **Establish the amount of funds initially available.** Many start-up initiatives start with the needs or expenses first, but one really must consider what funds are in existence first. Then, build a budget that will cover the costs of transitioning a space. For a home, these transition costs can be substantial, so a prioritization of what expenses are critically necessary to satisfy code requirements, contractual obligations. In any regard, if possible, the opening of the center should not commence until the first full year of operational expenses have been established. This will ease the pressure once the center opens. It's difficult enough to manage new volunteer and client procedures without having to

manage new fund-raising as well. The A Baby's Breath model has only one main fund-raiser per center so that we are an organization of offering free services and not an organization of raising money.

3) **Train your board.** Unless one is blessed with the perfect constellation of leaders and volunteers, the first board must do the initial work of the volunteers. I had to learn this the hard way, but since there was no A Baby's Breath initially, I was all the volunteers and the board all in one. With every new center that was developed, I got a little smarter about how much of my personal time I invested. If there's too much dependence in the development, then the expectation is that contribution of time will continue after the center opens. I've also learned on more than one occasion that the fund-raising procedures need to be learned by the board. That way, the board can educate others in the fund-raising procedures if they must be retaught. The most successful centers we have started have had their boards directly involved with the fund-raisers.

4) **Training is an ongoing process.** Every client and volunteer should be considered a lesson. Our initial training at A Baby's Breath started with thirty-two candidates, and nine months later, there was only one. We've tinkered with a couple of different time lines and materials. We ended up with an amalgamation of materials, but a time line of about six weeks. That is more than enough time to figure out if a candidate can work. A Baby's Breath has a cycle of training starting with open houses in the fall and ending with a Leadership course. We've been able to refresh our boards, volunteers and leaders every year in this way.

Opening One's Center

1) **The initial challenge** Keeping volunteers who have come through training active until the client base builds is the initial challenge. If the volunteers don't see a client immediately, he/she might think there's no need for the service/center. There's lot of non-client work to be done—finding new resources in the area, establishing a Baby Store, praying for our future clients, advertising the center. Until the word gets out in the community about what the center does, it will be a challenge to keep volunteers feeling like their time is well spent.
2) **Starting a client base** - What I did at A Baby's Breath was to reach out to a local practitioner's office. I was given her client list and started calling clients directly to see if they needed help. Initially, these clients would just come for the baby things. The taxicabs would pull up, the trunk would open, and we would load them up with anything they saw and needed. At times, our supply of baby items went down to nothing as the need outpaced the supply. It was frustrating for me personally, however, because I wanted a way to work with the clients. It wasn't until we established the Baby Store that we could spend time and establish goals for our clients.
3) **Advertising**—One must have some way to spread the word out to one's potential clients. We initially made a brochure at A Baby's Breath that looked like a scientific rationalization of an unborn baby. It really didn't give potential clients any idea of what we

could do for them. Over the years, we have illustrated and documented the services that we do offer. However, we have found it a challenge to get our secular partners to accept what we do. Many times, crisis centers are listed as support services and not "pregnancy counseling." This is because many do not consider us as a place that offers all the "choices." This is true. We are transparent in everything we do at A Baby's Breath. We are about the life choices, helping mothers and fathers in crisis pregnancies.

BUDGET

1) **The main expenses of a center** Rental contracts, insurance policies, utilities are the operational expenses and if one's organization is mostly volunteer like ours was and is, they are the only obstacles to keeping the doors open. Since our organization has grown to five centers, we share the cost of the insurance among them so that our ultrasound centers are not burdened with the entire cost of our malpractice insurance. Our cell phone costs are also shared, and we have an attractive contract with Verizon for all our cell and landline needs. We also cover the consultant fees for individuals who administer help for the organization. If only one center is operating alone, however, all those operational costs need to be covered by the outcome of one's fund-raiser.

2) **Establishing one fund-raiser** Establishing one's fund-raiser is starting one's initial base of support. We have a way to accept donations online called an Angel Club and a silent auction for our shared costs, but the local fund-raiser is key to establishing stability and consistency for one's organization. We do not consider fund-raiser programs that offer less than a 50 percent return. We've been asked many times to participate in various fund-raisers, and we pick and choose which ones with which to be connected. For "fund-raisers" with returns less than 50 percent, it's really about PR. One word of caution about these less-than-50-percent-return fund-raisers: if one is not careful about receiving the money, one's name is being used for the

merchant's advertising. A Baby's Breath established the Run for Life as its primary way to support a center. The Run for Life is comparatively easy to organize, and the sponsors that support a center one year can be solicited the following year. Our Run for Life at the Norristown Farm Park is on its twentieth year, and it's been successful in large part due to the leadership of Dorothy Swedkowski and her husband Bud. They have enlisted the support of the Knights of Columbus, from church, and from the local CYO teams to create places where life can be chosen.

The silent auction and golf outing are great ways to raise large sums of money, but they are more burdensome to manage. We had initially been dependent upon a Run for Life and a silent auction for the first five years, but after that, as we expanded into three centers, we needed another form of support. We now use the silent auction to cover our shared expenses of cell phones, insurance, and consultant stipends. The silent auction chair, Maria Diesel, does an amazing job in managing an efficient fund-raiser. The golf outing chairs, Marsha Warner and John Baldassari, were successful in their chairing the last two outings. Proceeds from our first two outings went toward the transition costs of our home, but now go toward the Independence program, which helps clients transition into a lifestyle that is independent of government support and does not produce crisis pregnancies.

3) **Financial Independence from other like-minded organizations**
When considering church-based financial support, one should keep in mind that an established church is its own faith-based organization. That church has its own operational costs, and one cannot really depend upon it blindly. This was the recommended approach by another pregnancy help center that I initially considered before starting A Baby's Breath. The plan was to lock into an agreement with a church so that no other pregnancy help center could share the donors. It is unfortunate, because this is what creates the hostility between help centers. While we are very noncompetitive in our approach, we believe that through our

model more people can be helped for less. There literally could be an A Baby's Breath in every church.

4) **The ideal fund-raising model** - We have tried several different approaches to planning an annual fund-raiser and we've established a Run for Life at each center due to its ease of execution and our ability to recreate it every year. It also produces almost all our needed income for a center for the entire year. At our Jeffersonville center, about ten consistent annual sponsors have been the reason for that center's existence for the past seventeen years. I thought this would be an easy thing to establish at our wealthier community centers, but it is not. Our most difficult center to establish was our Main Line center. We had initially given that center $20,000 to start and then went back to try and teach them the methods of executing a Run for Life. For the past ten years, since opening our first Main Line center, we have had to retrain a different group of people every year.

Maintaining a Center

1) **Annual Leadership training** - Volunteers come through our leaders who we train/retrain at an annual leadership course. The shared leadership is responsible for conducting the specific training needed at their centers. The best way to create consistency is to hold the open houses in the fall when the children go back to school, moms have more time to devote to causes, and people are back from their summer vacations. After the initial volunteer training, all volunteers are invited to a leadership course. At the leadership course, individual volunteers learn what it takes to be a leader. Many are surprised at the scope of the leadership positions and are encouraged to consider that position if it opens. We had a transition needed at our Jeffersonville center. An advocate, Kate Chetta, attended the director training, and when that director needed to step down, Kate knew what was required of her to execute her tasks.
2) **Advocate and board meetings are separate meetings for a reason**. Not all board members are interested getting involved with clients' issues. Board meetings are about keeping the doors open and issues with volunteers or clients, but not about individual clients' progress toward goals. Advocate meetings are ideally held once per month. When I was director, I used to have a Mass at the center. It was a great way to connect with the advocates spiritually. Once cannot underestimate the amount of grace needed by a crisis center. I recommend some form

of prayer, Bible study, or rosary every month for the group of people who are ministering to our clients. I've personally held a weekly Adoration Hour at my local church for the past eighteen years that has given me the grace to execute and grow A Baby's Breath.

3) **Established communication** - Board meetings should be regular, but as I mention in the Communication section—it's whatever works for one's organization. Once one has a framework for administering services and conducting fund-raisers, it might not be necessary to do more than one or two a year. Even as a corporate board, we hold one in the beginning of the year to affirm our budget and then just have a profit and loss sent to all board members monthly to make sure we are paying our bills and our funds are meeting our expenses.

4) **Financial reporting** Understanding one's spending habits is critical. Our organization hit some bumps until we could get financial reporting to happen regularly. We had a volunteer, Chris Cusatis (God rest his soul), who helped us establish our system of recording incomes/expenses into funds. Each fund represents a center/service. We could properly monitor the incomes/expenses and plan and prepare for each year, center, and service. Janet Bizal and Cathy Janoson are the current keepers of the finances at A Baby's Breath. The way that the funds are organized helps the centers understand how much money they have at any given time and what the expected outcomes should be for their centers to be operational.

5) **Record keeping** - Our client reporting comes through the website database but needs additional manicuring from human help. We have a variety of skill sets at A Baby's Breath. It does not require a PhD to care about a client, so we have many advocates who sometimes do not collect information the same way as those who are compensated for their time. The information that we like to see collected is about clients' goals. The advocate is managing their emotional health, and sometimes it is a challenge for them to collect data on the clients' progress. We persevere in gathering this information, however, because it is important to encourage

someone who is in a crisis to see the end of the tunnel. The client reports are valuable to the board, who are sometimes results-oriented and like to see the outcome of their time. They are also valuable for showing the outcomes of any grant writing efforts.

A Baby's Breath—Social Services Structure – Key Positions

Core Services Center (offering pregnancy counseling, prenatal/parenting classes, tutoring with a Baby Store)

Center Director:

General Manager:

Donations Coordinator:

Run for Life Director:
Day of the Run Coordinator:
Run for Life Staff:
Prenatal Class Nurse Instructors:
Parenting Class Coordinator:
Baby Store Coordinator:
Advocates:
Tutors:

KAREN JANE PATOTA, FOUNDER

Core Services Center with Ultrasound Services

Center Director:

General Manager:

Donations Coordinator:

Run for Life Director:
Day of the Run Coordinator:
Run for Life Staff:
Ultrasound Nurse/Tech:
Medical Director:
Radiologist:
Prenatal Class Nurse Instructors:
Parenting Class Coordinator:
Baby Store Coordinator:
Advocates:
Tutors:

Core Services Center with Housing Services

Center Director (and Housing Board):

General Manager:

Donations Coordinator:

Run for Life Director:
Day of the Run Coordinator:
Run for Life Staff:
Prenatal Class Nurse Instructors:
Parenting Class Coordinator:
Baby Store Coordinator:
Advocates:
House Mom:
Tutors:

KAREN JANE PATOTA, FOUNDER

Core Services Center with Natural Family Planning, Loving our Life, The Rose Garden, or Any Helpful Social Service Coordinators

Center Director:

General Manager:

Donations Coordinator:

Run for Life Director:
Day of the Run Coordinator:
Run for Life Staff:
Prenatal Class Nurse Instructors:
Parenting Class Coordinator:
Baby Store Coordinator:
Advocates:
Tutors:
Natural Family Planning Instructors, Loving our Life Coordinators, The Rose Garden or Other Social Services Coordinators:

How to Create Compassionate Places - Lessons for All Faith-Based Social Service Organizations

Service

> **For as the body without the spirit is dead,**
> **so faith without works is dead also.**
> —James 2:26

Faith is a very abstract concept to explain. For some it is a generic belief in a higher being, and for others it becomes personal conviction that Jesus Christ has saved his or her soul. For those outside a faithful existence, understanding the concept of faith can be a challenge. If one is to implement a faith-based social service, the agreement is that faith is the driving force behind the actions of the individual and for the entire organization.

Some faith-based organizations require an affirmation of salvation by the individual and the organization. The organization by its actions is the end process of salvation. The donors to such organizations are delivering faith by proxy.

For the Catholic faith-based service, the service is an outcome of our faith, and it is faith sharing as opposed to delivering faith. The donors to Catholic social services expect the services to be delivered in accordance with their faith's principles, but are not necessarily considering their actions as salvific. Catholic donors expect their money to facilitate a good and do not necessarily expect a salvation to take place unless the recipient feels the love of God at hand.

C. S. Lewis, in his first definition of faith,[14] describes it as something that grows as one with God's plan. As I grew from an individual just trying to choose God's plan personally to an individual trying to help others choose their own plan, I created a group of individuals banded together trying to pull people to the love of God.

The type of social service that I chose to develop was moral in nature. There was a right and wrong choice to make in the choice for abortion. The right choices to make follow God's law, but the clients that we help with our organization come from a number of different faith

---

14 C. S. Lewis, *Mere Christianity* (New York: Touchstone, 1996), page 123-127.

backgrounds, so it is not ours to judge whether or not they are sinners. We help clients whether or not they are sinners. We don't make anyone feel guilty for the decisions they've made in the past, but we don't represent a choice that is not of our beliefs. We represent the choices for life.

The clients who we've tried to help were choosing a lifestyle that would produce crisis pregnancies. Their lifestyle would also create uncertainty in the future, lack of self-respect, and really no direction in life. There are many reasons why clients choose that lifestyle, and all of them relate back to a lack of faith—in themselves and in God.

A large majority of the volunteers at A Baby's Breath, including myself, have lived through a time where they were outside their faith. They experienced firsthand the lack of respect, self-esteem, and the abyss without the love of God. That is the reason they are compelled to sacrifice their time, talent, and treasure to be with our clients. They are there because they care, and for no other reason. There are no paychecks for service at A Baby's Breath, and that's to show our clients that it is God's love that we are sharing.

>Questions:
>What is the motivation for one's organization in doing a service?
>What gifts can the workers of the organization share with clients?
>Does the organization expect clients to change immediately with one's help?
>Does the organization feel a responsibility to one's donors to act on their behalf?

KAREN JANE PATOTA, FOUNDER

Mercy

> **For why should I judge outsiders? Is it not your business to judge those within? God will judge those outside.**
> —1 Corinthians (5:12–13)

Corporal works of Mercy are acts that provide material goods or comfort to those in need. The US government does this with a social security check or welfare assistance. There is no moral guidance associated with this form of support. It is given to prevent starvation, to clothe the naked, and to house widows and orphans, but it is certainly not predicated on a condition of faith or to change their lifestyle or to give a moral direction.

Spiritual works of Mercy are those acts that help sinners understand their faith. Sometimes the sinner is so mired down in sin that he or she can't see what Truth is. This is the job of faith-based organizations—to teach the Truth. It's not enough to have people in that organization that have faith; the mission of a faith-based organization should teach what is right or wrong.

Mother Teresa's Sisters of Charity organization is a perfect combination of both spiritual and corporal works of Mercy. Mother Teresa taught about Jesus by saying that if you judge people, you have no time to love them.

A Baby's Breath teaches the law through kindness as well. Our advocates are like Mother Teresa in not judging but helping them understand the right direction in life. We clothe the naked, feed the hungry, and teach about Jesus by example.

Mother Teresa's critics usually measured her success on "results." The statistics of how many mouths she could feed, or her ability to control the number of mouths in the future were an inaccurate measure of her worth. She said God does not require us to be successful, only to be faithful. I can't count the times I have repeated this expression with regard to the "results" of our success at A Baby's Breath. If the definition of "success" is the number of babies we have saved, we couldn't take credit for those saves even if we could count them. The choice for life rests entirely on the mother and the grace of God. She may have influences in her life that are greater than our support, she might have doctors or organizations that are convincing her that she is doing the "right" thing for the child, or she could willingly be committing a sin. We can't control that—not even God can; we all have free will.

Our success at A Baby's Breath is to provide support to those who are choosing life, to provide training for advocates who want to help, and to facilitate the means of support for mothers, fathers, and families choosing life.

Mother Teresa evidenced her moral teaching when asked, as she often was, because she became so well-respected for her love. A Baby's Breath has become well-respected for our love of our clients. We treat our clients with respect, and with that they know more about the God we love.

For any faith-based organization, your actions are those of Jesus. Through the loving, compassionate help you give, you should allow your clients to see, hear, and feel the actions and Word of Jesus.

Questions:
    Does one's organization have a moral order?
    How will one's organization teach compassion?
    If clients ask for moral direction, how would one's workers respond?

Mission

> **I am the Alpha and Omega.**
> —Revelations 1:8

What is the need in one's community, and how can one's organization best be of service? Those questions should be answered by one's mission statement. In the case of A Baby's Breath, the need was for a crisis pregnancy center. We had a Respect Life group that had a common philosophy, and we needed a direction. The mission began with the goal "to help a mother to see her child take his/her first breath."

Every mission should have a charter, and we replicated ours from another crisis pregnancy center. The reason why we chose not to adopt the other organization's mission was because it limited our scope and our charter. The other organization's mission focused primarily on the choice of life, but we wanted to address the reasons why a mother or father would be in a crisis pregnancy.

We thought that education had something to do with a mother feeling ill-equipped to parent, so we added the educational needs of clients to our charter.

We also thought that a mother's choices before becoming pregnant should be addressed in a change of lifestyle. We didn't want to be the type of organization that merely gives a packet of pills to a client, and then hope that the client finds the ideal relationship through a physical relationship first. We then adopted a position against using artificial contraceptives.

Given my personal experiences with relationships that lack commitment, I also understood that the clients we would serve needed to be gently guided toward relationships that were mutual. We advocated for committed Christian relationships.

The reason why we prioritized our mission over the other aspects of our charter was because the choice of life is absolute. Abortion is always a wrong, but abstinence is relative. Sometimes our clients are married, so abstinence (the only absolute way to prevent pregnancy) is not an option all the time—it's relative. If a crisis pregnancy occurs in a marriage, the options for managing that crisis pregnancy are much better because there are two individuals with the same goal of parenting.

We chose to celebrate chastity as a positive "affirmation of someone who knows how to live self-giving, free from any self-centered slavery."[15] We offer support to single people who are choosing a Christian lifestyle, and advise our crisis clients to make choices that will not result in a crisis pregnancy, but our priority continues to be to directly help mothers and fathers in crisis pregnancies—before, during and after.

The first and last consideration to one's mission is God. How is the organization going to serve God? We thought about who we are as a group and who we wanted to help. While we were Catholics and Christians united by our baptisms, we wanted to help people of all faiths, and we didn't want volunteers or clients to receive their confirmation in Christ through us. We protected the choice of the individual to choose their church.

> Questions:
> For the mission—who will be helped?
> How will the organization help others?
> Why is the organization committed to this mission?

---

15 USCCB (www.usccb.org)

KAREN JANE PATOTA, FOUNDER

Transparency

> **Your light must shine before others, that they may see your good deeds and glorify your heavenly Father.**
> —Matthew 5:16

A name should describe the business as well as how one intends to operate. A supermarket might have a name to describe the fresh wholesome food it sells, or a car dealer's name would describe the cars and the honorable name that buyers could trust. With faith-based organizations it should be no different. A church name describes the patron saint or the way participants could expect to worship.

In the nonprofit world of crisis pregnancy centers, there is some debate about how an organization should advertise its name. Some pro-life groups have suggested that mothers and fathers in crisis don't need to know the way the organization operates. Some pro-abortion organizations think that the client should plan pregnancies when in fact abortion is their main business.

A Baby's Breath's name had its origins at Visitation B.V.M. Adoration Chapel in Trooper. I was given a copy of *Story of a Soul* by Saint Therese of Lisieux, "The Little Flower." I admired her greatly for the way she respected God and taught women how to act with reverence and obedience to Him. I wanted the organization to replicate her "little ways" of love. Baby's breath is a little flower and "The Little Flower" is our patron saint for A Baby's Breath.

There are some other considerations, like placement in the local business pages for alternatives to abortions, with A Baby's Breath topping all the competition. Since we are a faith-based organization, I prefer to think that the name that was being conferred upon our organization would evoke an emotion for those who said the words "A Baby's Breath." Just thinking about the sweet innocent smell of a baby's breath humanizes the baby that is held within.

Breath is another name for the Holy Spirit. The name A Baby's Breath reflects the nature of our business, which is to protect and care for the breathing of a baby like the breathing of God's spirit on this world.

We maintain the word "baby" in our name because we do not ignore the obvious reason why a mother or father is in crisis. It was suggested on a national pro-life website that no mother who was considering an abortion should be taken to a crisis center with the word "baby" in its name. We felt that the mother and father should be given a truthful response to the nature of our business and how we intended to operate.

A Baby's Breath Crisis Pregnancy Centers help mothers and fathers in crisis pregnancies. Truthful. Honest. Faithful.

Questions:
    How will people describe one's faith-based organization?
    How is God reflected in one's work?
    Could the organization's name change another's heart?

KAREN JANE PATOTA, FOUNDER

Humility

> **Grant that we may sit, one on Your right and one on Your left, in Your glory.**
> —Mark 10:37

Starting a faith-based organization is a grand and ambitious endeavor. The mission in place, the initial group of people are banded together for the life of the organization—or so it seems. There are many obstacles and battles along the way to achieving stability at first. There are logistical issues involving how the organization functions, including where it will be located, what the name will be, and who will be helped. All the details are usually decided upon by the main driver of the organization—the founder.

The founder will be the primary decision-maker and thereby receive the accolades of successfully starting a faith-based organization but also bear the brunt of the criticism. He or she will persevere through many trials, as was the case with A Baby's Breath. It all started with four people sitting around my kitchen table, but seventeen years later, only one other founding board member survived the trials and tribulations of starting an organization.

I think the first major debate was how the money from the fundraiser was to be distributed. One of the initial board members wanted this money to go toward a family who had lost a loved one. The fundraising committee even wanted to change the name of the run to include the lost loved one's name. When the initial board members decided that this was not a good idea, the split began between the main fund-raiser and the founder. It ended two and a half years later with the main fund-raiser quitting just months before the event. It was a precursor to how this organization would encounter and survive turmoil.

A Baby's Breath was a much-needed service, so the organization grew to having three centers in just five years. Initially, we had tried to function with one main board, but the day-to-day issues were given to a locally based director. In the fifth year of operation, the organization tried to split into local boards of governing. This was another extremely hard lesson to learn for the founder. We had appointed directors one after the other until a system of training came about (see the section on Leadership).

One center had a very good leader who stepped up after the first one quit. She was kind and soft-spoken, but had great organizational skills. She learned what I was trying to teach her, but she had her own unique, innate gifts that could not have been taught by anyone but God. She was well loved by her clients and her volunteers. The only issue that she was having was finding a group of people who would devote themselves to the task of funding the budget for that center completely.

Many boards of faith-based and nonprofit organizations place an extremely heavy burden on their Executive director (one main executive). What I had found in my experience of being both president and director is that there were certain tasks that involved people, tasks that had to do with fundraising, and the record-keeping tasks. I could separate what I had done for the whole organization into three main categories of leadership—a director, a general manager, and a donations coordinator. The shared leadership created a balance of power and made administering services possible – even with transitions.

The local boards of A Baby's Breath are divided into thirds, with each board position coinciding with a leadership position, sharing the role of administrating each center/service. For example, the race director position is one most associated with the general management position because it helps to raise money for the organization. The prenatal/parenting class coordinator positions are most closely associated with the director position because they are working with volunteers and clients. We are selective with who has access to our database, but anyone who does have it is helping the Donations Coordinator position in updating our records. The other jobs that were helpful to implement services were not necessarily board positions, but if they wanted to participate in fund-raising (as all boards must do), they could be on the local center/service board.

Questions:
    What jobs are critically necessary to administrate the services offered by the organization?
    Can these jobs be designated to one of the three main leadership positions?
    What are the expectations of each position?

Leadership

> I am the Way, the Truth and the Life; no one
> comes to the Father but through Me.
> —John 14:6

A faith-based organization should be a living tutorial on how to love God through Word and action.

I will specifically address the organizations that are primarily volunteer-based because that is the success to which I can attest, but even a compensated worker in a faith-based organization should espouse the qualities of Christ. A faith-based organization will attract volunteers (workers) from every skill set, educational background, and previous life experience. Some be highly educated in social work; some will have great financial wizardry. Others will come with a high school education and a fantastic manner with volunteers and clients. The challenge that a faith-based organization faces is that it should accept all forms of help. Unless the volunteer is belligerent, derogatory against the organization or management, or is a criminal, we must accept his or her help.

As the faith-based organization is forming, it is a little difficult to see the roses among the daisies (the people that should be leaders, volunteers working with clients, and volunteers who should stay in the fundraising circles). Some leaders are the daisies—it's not about a judgment of character or skill, but an honest assessment of how the individual can help or hinder an organization. What we have done at A Baby's Breath is to give each volunteer or worker the chance to prove himself or herself. Sometimes it takes a little time before we can see how a person acts in a faith-based position.

All leaders need to have the following:

1) **Humility**—God is the victor in the success of faith-based organizations. This needs to be understood by one's leaders, or the success could be misconstrued as their own. Donors are investing in a cause—not necessarily in the person running the organization.

2) **Strength**—Many challenges confront a faith-based organization. A firm backbone helps to make good decisions, even when the pressure is on to cave into an expedient decision that compromises the integrity of the organization. For example, we take a position against the use of artificial contraceptives. We do this because it's the lifestyle that is the problem—not the baby (or babies). A mother who refuses to change her lifestyle will bear the burden of the decision to be sexually active. Whether parenting or choosing adoption, a mother who continues to find herself in crisis pregnancies will have the financial burden of managing children of whom she cannot afford. While choosing the adoption path is an honorable and loving option, the end does not justify the means. It is still a difficult decision. The abortion decision is not an option, but no contraceptive method is foolproof or without risk of a sexually transmitted disease. We have had volunteers who have taken it upon themselves to take a client to have her tubes tied. The result is one of remorse in not adhering to our policy, but it takes a strong leader to say no. The success of our mission and its growth have not suffered for standing up for Catholic–Christian principles against the use of contraceptives. The volunteer who is not strong in her respect for our mission usually leaves of her own accord.

3) **Wisdom**—"Fear of God is the beginning of wisdom" (Prov. 9:10). While we are compassionate in our approach, leaders of faith-based organizations especially need to act upon their moral compass while in this position. The challenges can come in many forms. While starting the organization, I found it very difficult to manage the stress of the organization and my family. There were many times when I asked myself and my husband, "Is this worth it?" My husband supported the sacrifice of time and mental energy and the added financial help that would have been available if I accepted any compensation, but I just couldn't take money from A Baby's Breath. It wasn't a personal fear that drove me to sacrifice so much as that the solution to abortion needed to be a big sacrifice. Providing alternatives to abortion is helping to save souls—not just that of the baby, but of the mother and father in a crisis pregnancy as well.

4) **Detachment of Self**—This is closely related to the humility attribute that every leader should espouse. Anger and frustration are usually a sign that someone has too much invested in the mission. I found myself—many times—angry at volunteers, a setback in our progress, but never toward clients. Clients need compassion, not anger. I've had leaders who initially thought they had what it takes to deal with a client's lack of progress who found themselves personally invested in the client's success, lashing out when the client did not meet the leader's ideal of success. This is not a good leader, and the organization should do everything possible to protect clients from this type of leader. Another example of detachment is the success of finances or the results of one's mission. One must remember that it is God's success and victory; the leader or individual contributor is just the instrument. If a fund-raiser is a success, God made it succeed. If a client achieves her goals, it's through the grace of God that she has done this.

5) **Living the Lifestyle**—A Baby's Breath is a goal-oriented organization, and one of those goals is to not have a client return in another crisis pregnancy. It would seem that given those goals, we would receive volunteers and leaders who are familiar with achieving a lifestyle that is congruent with no possibility of a crisis pregnancy (i.e., a chaste lifestyle), but we have had potential volunteers and leaders who think they can teach chastity while not living it. This will not work. If one's organization is about teaching morality, its teachers should be morally bound.

Questions:

What does one's organization stand for in terms of values?

How can the organization protect one's clients from the possibility that leaders or volunteers are not the people they advertised on their volunteer agreement forms?

How can the organization transition a bad leader or volunteer?

Training Leaders

> **So then it does not depend on the man who wills or the man who runs, but on God who has mercy.**
> —Romans 9:16

What is the reason for your organization? If it is a faith-based one, then the reason is to serve God's purpose. Workers in your organization should have this as their primary motivation for being a part of your organization. It should not be compensation, convenience, or the potential for recognition of doing something great. All those things may or may not be a part of a worker's experience with your organization, but if they become the primary reason, there might be problems down the road. For example, if the compensation is not enough, suddenly the convenience might not be there. The currency of your workers is doing God's will and being what God wills them to be. Any other motivation will be tested, as many faith-based organizations can attest. The success of any faith-based organization should be accredited to God's victory alone. We are just the instruments.

Training leaders and preparing for transition is a constant battle in the world of faith-based organizations (I am told it is also a challenge in secular business as well). It has been by the grace of God that our organization has grown from one center to five in fifteen years. It has required a constant effort to teach, reteach, and retrain leaders.

The leaders at A Baby's Breath teach the individual volunteers through the everyday operations, advocate meetings, and also acquire new volunteers every year through open houses. If volunteers demonstrate responsibility and a willingness to do more, we invite them to a leadership course.

The A Baby's Breath leadership course was developed after running three centers, and it was through this course that the two additional centers were created. Our format has a segment that addresses all volunteers and then has breakout sessions that hone the skills needed to execute the services, provide the funding, and update all leadership positions with changes in procedures or policies. At the end of the day, the course is organized by the local center or service boards.

In addition to the five centers that have been created, we have added a medical service of executing ultrasounds, a service to provide support for singles choosing to live a Christian lifestyle, a free natural family planning service, a support group for couples ready to adopt, and the most recent addition, a housing service to provide a temporary home for homeless pregnant moms, and a job training service.

It should be mentioned, however, that the leadership course is the beginning of the leadership tenure at A Baby's Breath. There's not enough time to devote to every aspect of the job, but a leadership checklist is provided so that the leader trainee has an idea of the expectations of his or her position. I found that if I didn't list out all of the jobs that could potentially be associated with a leadership position, when a new job was added it was not well received. It's better for the leadership to know that the expectations of a leadership position could grow than to let the leader think that whatever the leader can do is acceptable. Whatever doesn't get done by a leader floats its way up the top executive position/board.

Considerations:
    Develop a checklist for the leadership positions.
    Decide if the job is a people-oriented job, a money-related job, or a record-keeping job.
    Develop a plan for ongoing education in case of transitions.

Competition

> **But I say to you, love your enemies and
> pray for those who persecute you.**
> —Matthew 5:4

Just imagine the outcome if more nonprofit social services had this as their goal: helping more people for less. This is the goal at A Baby's Breath. We have exceptional people who have donated their time and talent to us. I believe it's because we operate with a volunteer management structure that allows us to execute a budget that would be comparable to a Boy Scout pack budget. Social services should have a different model than one used for "for-profit" business. The model of A Baby's Breath maximizes the number of people helped by sharing the precious resources that are available to help our clients. We don't have the competition factor, as many nonprofits do. We share, and the benefit is that more people are helped.

A Baby's Breath began without the support of the local pro-life organization, but it was not insurmountable. What opposition we had only made our organization stronger in its ability to survive. We were denied access to the immediate and more readily available pro-life funds, so we had to develop our own mechanism of support. I really didn't like to fund-raise; I would rather work directly with clients, so the system of A Baby's Breath is very streamlined and independent of government, church, or pro-life group support. We create a sponsorship of people who want to see what we offer available to those in their communities. We still do get church, pro-life, and sometimes pro-choice support, but we do not accept government support. Government support is a trap for a compromise of principle. I have seen organizations that do accept government support wallow in bloated budgets and give up the whole reason for their existence, which is to teach faith.

Sharing resources is not the only form of competition in a faith-based world. It's also about sharing volunteers. A Baby's Breath does not have a noncompete clause in our volunteer agreement. If a volunteer feels called to work at multiple organizations—pro-life or not—it's not our decision to make. We are confident in our ability to sustain ourselves and trust that God will reward us for sharing.

My partner at A Baby's Breath, J. B., has at times had to remind me that if the mission of another organization is in keeping with ours, we are brothers in Christ. Prayers for the people who persecute us should be reserved for the organizations that defile the sanctity of human life.

Questions:
   Who is the organization's base of support?
   Are the available funds targeted by another organization similar to one's mission?
   Understand the differences between organizations so that if possible a partnership can be formed.

Problem Volunteers

> **For many are called, but few are chosen.**
> —Matthew 22:14

The service of God is a chosen path, but many who are called to do His work. So what do you do when someone who chooses your organization is not working out? Do we have to choose back? I have come to learn that it is best to try to find a place in the organization that works for an individual if possible.

1) **Disrespectful of Leadership**—This quality comes in many forms. It could be a volunteer who publicly criticizes the leaders or how the organization functions. I had one board member who was extremely difficult to deal with. This individual was very good a targeting me for disrespect, and when it was time for a decision on where this individual would best serve the organization, I was at a loss as to educate everyone on how toxic her relationship was with me and with the organization. Retrospectively speaking, I should have requested help from my board about the individual's actions, but at the time I was not able to communicate well about issues. Instead, I fired the individual from the board, and it led to a great deal of angst across the board. The perception was that I was overzealous in my leadership, and there was sympathy for the disrespectful volunteer. It's never a comfortable situation to talk openly at a board meeting, but sometimes that is the only way to figure out the truth of the situation. Board meetings should be a safe zone where anyone can offer up ideas, suggestions, or issues. Managing the tone and objectivity of the issues should be the goal outcome of disputes, and giving people an opportunity to volunteer their time in another capacity should be offered to create space between individuals who aren't working well together.

2) **Disregarding the Mission and Charter of the Organization**—This is closely related to the first sign of disrespect, because it is disrespectful to ignore the will of the organization through its

mission. A Baby's Breath has in its mission and charter a position against contraception. We've had several volunteers who've disregarded these tenets and referred clients to get tubal ligations. When this happens, it is unexpected. As it was in our case, the volunteers usually left of their own volition, but it can be very disruptive for the volunteer leaders who are trying to execute the mission and charter. Therefore, is it extremely important to pick leaders well and to allow leaders in your organization who are devoted to your mission.

3) **Disrespecting Clients and Volunteers**—It is a good policy to observe your leaders in action. I was at one of our centers where a director was screaming at a client. She was telling her to get a job. While finding a job is a good objective for a client, screaming at her in a public way is never a good approach. This same director was also very caustic with volunteers, and many volunteers left because of her. It's never a good time to let go of a leader because of the potential disruption in services. It's always best to try to work with the leader/volunteer in a private setting, and when all else fails, bring it to the board's attention.

4) **Ineptitude**—Every faith-based organization has its strengths and weaknesses. A Baby's Breath plans for this in its model by sharing the leadership positions. That way, if there is truly a case of a volunteer who can't perform every aspect of a position, there is flexibility in sharing of the responsibilities. The only reason to dismiss someone who is not doing his or her job is if it's intentional, and the volunteer does not agree to delegate parts of his or her position that would better be done by someone else. If a volunteer doesn't work in one job, there is always a place at God's table.

5) **Not Showing Up**—If there's no paycheck, there's only the integrity of the individual. The integrity of the organization is reliant upon the leaders and volunteers showing up to administer the services. A Baby's Breath builds into its training program a way to vet volunteers who may not be the best to put in front of clients. We're trying to model responsible behavior at A Baby's Breath, and the clients who don't show up for their appointments are

not considered clients after two no-show visits. Half the battle of getting through crisis is being where one needs to be at a specific time and place. The goal of any faith-based organization should be to just be there.

Questions:
What are the critical goals of the organization?
How can one's organization strengthen its ability to control the actions of its workers?
How important is it to have the leaders of one's organization reflect Christian values?

Communication

> **Seeing that His divine power has granted to us everything pertaining to life and godliness, through the true knowledge of Him who called us by His own glory and excellence.**
> —2 Peter 1:3

God gives us what we need—this is how we have survived in our mission "to help a mother to see his/her first breath." If we had made stringent requirements about meetings every month or a specific number of people on our boards, we would have never started the first center.

A Baby's Breath grew from just four people at my kitchen table. While we strive to have a quorum of six at our corporate board meetings, we are only able to manage one or two meetings per year. From this annual meeting, we approve a budget for the entire organization and delegate down to the local centers the responsibility of managing the day-to-day finances and administration of services.

The local boards and services of A Baby's Breath are comprised of minimally three leaders, but anyone who wishes to be a part of the local boards can do so. The core members of director, general manager, and donations coordinator are the only required positions needed for financial decisions.

Advocate/volunteer meetings are the best way for the advocates to be informed of new policies and resources, but with the varied availability of the volunteers, e-mail communication is usually the way our centers communicate.

For communication with our donors, A Baby's Breath has used a variety of mediums. Facebook, LinkedIn, and Constant Contact are often used to advertise fund-raisers, volunteer needs, and occasionally a client testimonial.

It has been interesting to see how people like to communicate. Some donors only like one occasional e-mail, and some just like to tap into Facebook or LinkedIn for updates.

Questions:
> What information needs to be shared about one's organization – for boards, volunteers, donors, clients?
> Who's one's target audience for clients and donors?
> How much time does one's boards have to engage in communication?

Commencement of Creating Compassionate Places

Ideas for Social Services Using the A Baby's Breath Model

It is my hope that this book is not the ending or completion of a life's work, but the beginning many new books, works, centers, and services, God willing, in His name.

Potential ideas for new services applying the A Baby's Breath model (in addition to creating crisis pregnancy centers and homes), include:

Taking care of the elderly at home
Homes for children
Homes for the elderly
Schools—with God's values
Day care for autistic children
Work programs for special-needs children
Low-cost medical clinics
Low-cost chiropractic clinics
Organic farming
After-school sports programs for children
Nutrition centers—teaching kinesiology methods of treating diseases
Marriage-counseling centers
Low-cost legal aid

A Baby's Breath—Social Services Structure Applied – Key Positions

Center Director: for people oriented jobs – training/managing volunteers, working directly with clients

General Manager: managing the budget, developing a fundraiser/income, paying bills, reporting finances

Donations Coordinator: Record keeping/computer related functions

The other positions needed would be applicable to execution of services. (i.e. Teachers, Care givers, Doctors, Lawyers, Chiropractors, etc.)

The Blessings of a Good Life

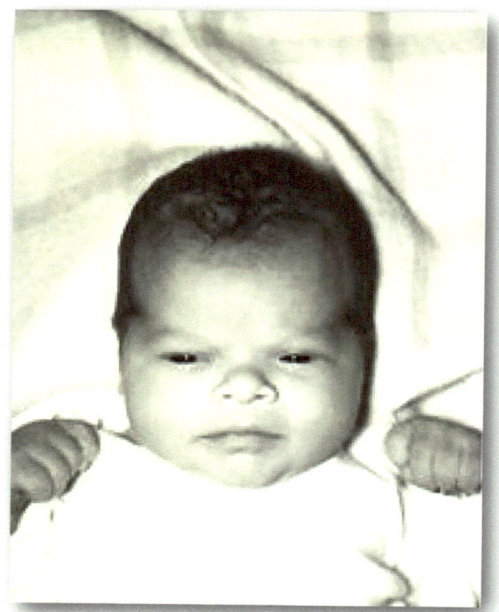

Figure 12- A Wanted Child born May 29, 1961

Figure 13- With Mom before Easter Mass

Figure 14 - First Holy Communion with my Mom

Figure 15 - First day of school

Figure 16- Third grade - loved school

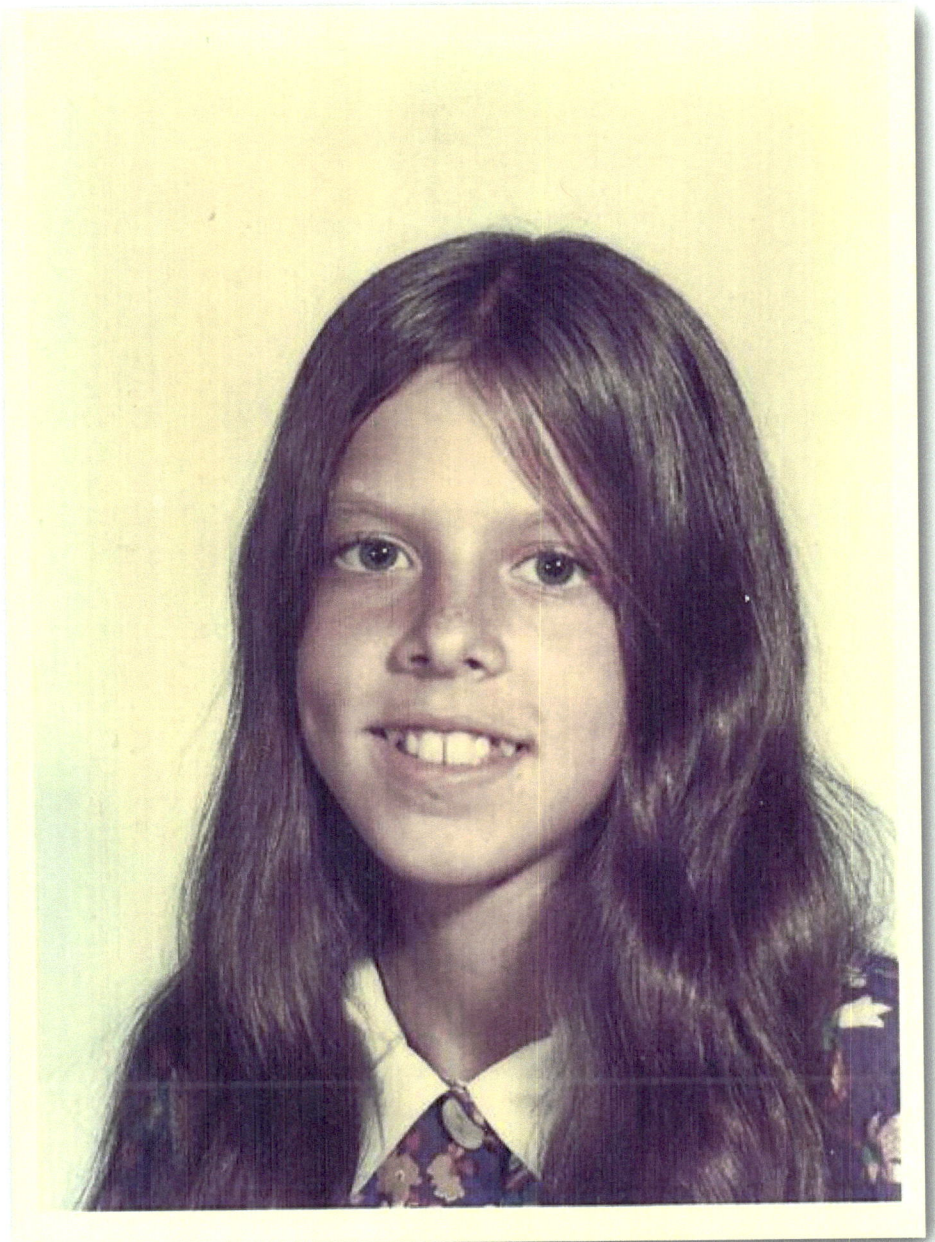

Figure 17- Sixth grade - Loved to laugh with my friends

Figure 18- Senior class picture - looking forward to graduating

Figure 19 - My sister stopped by to help me with my prom

CREATING COMPASSIONATE PLACES

Figure 20 - My brother John was there to share my joy of graduating

Figure 21 - Christmas before Josh was born

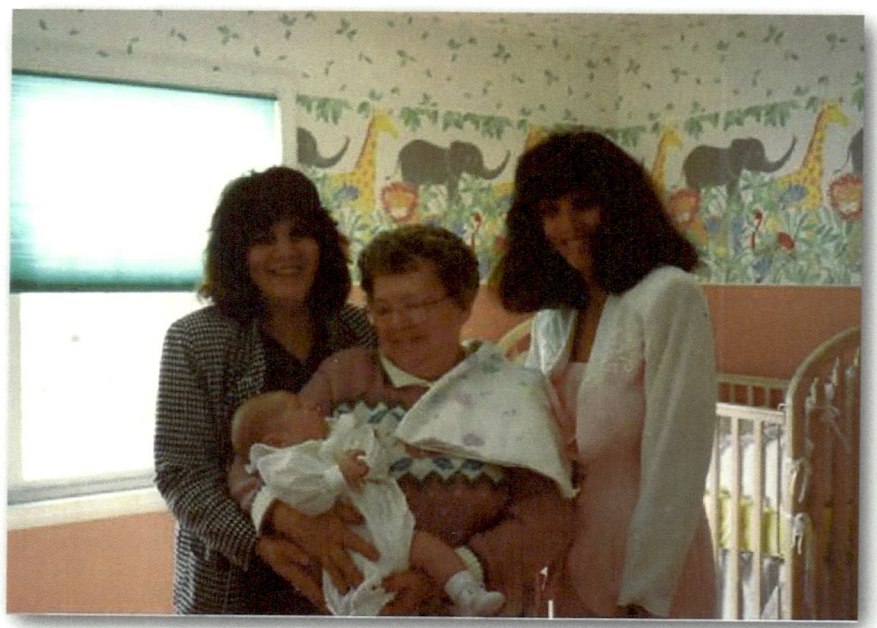

Figure 22- My Godmother, my sister Sue and my first baby, Josh

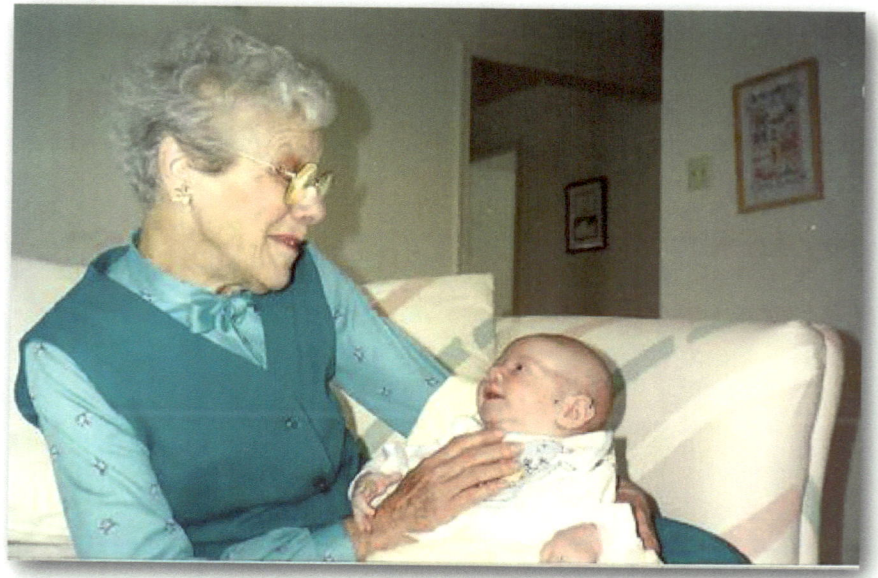

Figure 23 - All the great-grandchildren loved Great Grandmom

Figure 24- My 11 lb., 9 oz., Jared

Figure 25 - Father Navit proceeding over Jared's Baptism with his Godparents, Claire and Bobby Martorana

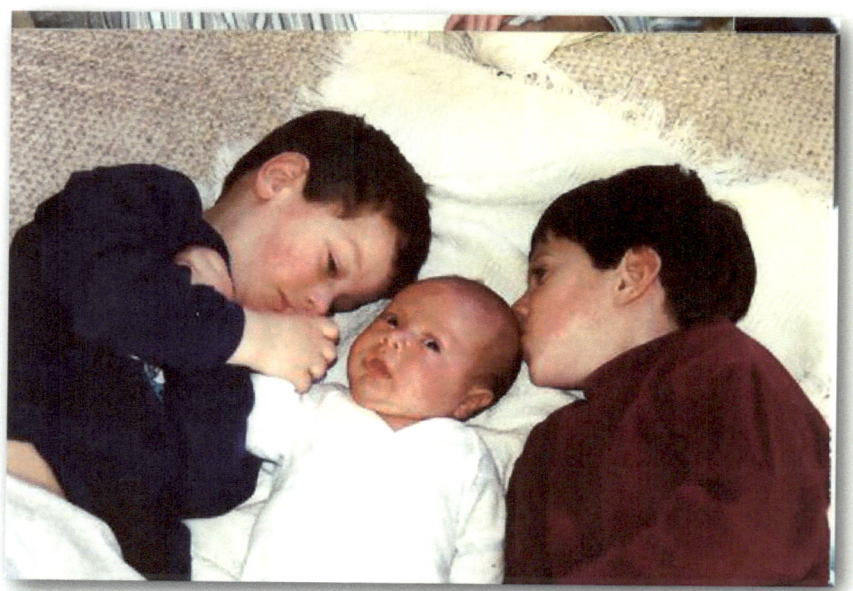

Figure 26- The Welcoming committee for Tom

Figure 27- My Dad with Tom

Figure 28- My blonde hair, blue eyed, Tom

Figure 29 - Victoria's Baptism -Amy and Eric Zaremski with Father Navit

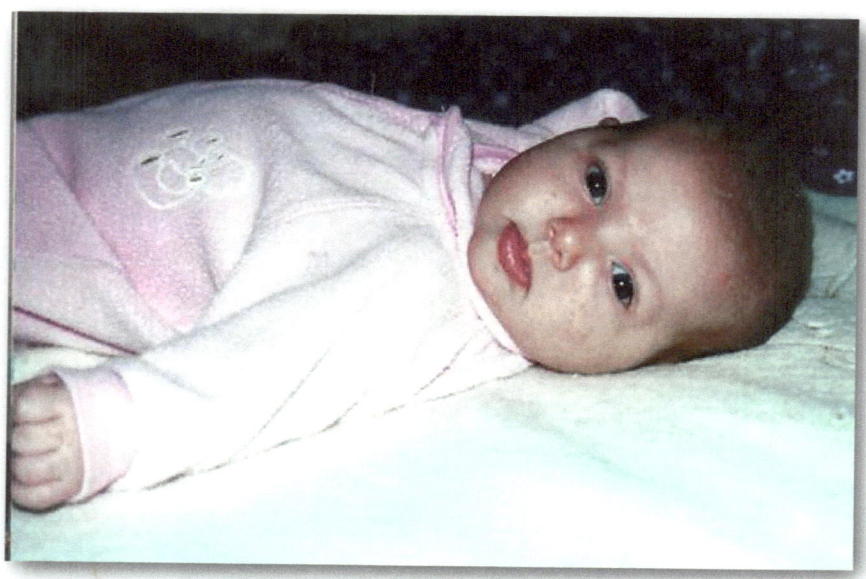

Figure 30- Pretty in pink, Victoria

CREATING COMPASSIONATE PLACES

Figure 31 - The Welcoming committee for Victoria

Figure 32 - A Swim day at Nana's pool

www.ingramcontent.com/pod-product-compliance
Lightning Source LLC
Chambersburg PA
CBHW042056290426
44111CB00001B/21